EDEXCEL
GCSE DRAMA

Study Guide

**RHIANNA ELSDEN,
ALICIA POPE,
DAVID PORTER** &
LUCY ELLEN RIX

rhinegold
EDUCATION

endorsed for
edexcel

First published 2016 in Great Britain by
Rhinegold Education
14-15 Berners Street
London W1T 3LJ, UK
www.rhinegoldeducation.co.uk

© 2016 Rhinegold Education
a division of Music Sales Limited

All rights reserved. No part of this publication may be reproduced, stored in a retrieval system, or transmitted in any form or by any means, electronic, mechanical, photocopying, recording or otherwise, without the prior permission of Rhinegold Education.

Rhinegold Education has used its best efforts in preparing this guide. It does not assume, and hereby disclaims, any liability to any party for loss or damage caused by errors or omissions in the guide whether such errors or omissions result from negligence, accident or other cause.

> You should always check the current requirements of your examination, since these may change.

Editor: Sarah Lambie
Consultant: Ed Boulter-Comer
Cover and book design: Fresh Lemon Australia

Edexcel GCSE Drama Study Guide
Order No. RHG370
ISBN: 978-1-78558-173-1

Exclusive Distributors:
Music Sales Ltd
Distribution Centre, Newmarket Road
Bury St Edmunds, Suffolk IP33 3YB, UK

Printed in the EU

Picture credits:
Alamy: 8 above (© Richard Garvey-Williams), 8 below, 27, 89 (© Lebrecht Music and Arts Photo Library), 9 © (Eric Nathan), 10 above (© Frances Roberts), 11 (© June Green), 14 (© LiliGraphie), (© Trigger Image), (© Filip Warulik), (© Blend Images), 21 (© Design Pics Inc.), 26 (© Mark Kelly), 31 (© GL Archive), (© Michael Dwyer), 48 & 49 (© WENN Ltd), 69 (© AF Archive), 118 & 124 (© Bettina Strenske), 155 (© Vicki Beaver), (© Jim West), (© Pxel), (© ipm), 161 (© Matthew Antonino), 170 (© Nick Scott). ArenaPAL: 38 (Frazer Ashford), 58 (Laurence Burns), 99, 106, 128 & 134 (Nigel Norrington), 109 (Robert Workman), 144 (Grigoriy Sisoev/RIA Novosti), 147 (Sheila Burnett), 167 (Johan Persson), 168 (Ullstein Bild). Catherine Ashmore: 78, 85. James Drawneek: 10. Manuel Harlan: 15. Isaac Lummis: 158. Helen Maybanks: 22. Claude Truong Ngoc: 18. REX Shutterstock: 12 (Ann Ward/Associated Newspapers), 35 (Jane Hobson), 114 & 158 (Alastair Muir). Steve Tanner: 42. TheHero: 29.

Contents

Introduction
Your GCSE course 5

The theatre
History of the theatre 8
Theatre layouts 10

Component 1: Devising
What does devising mean in drama? 12
Component 1: Key facts 13
Choice of stimuli 14
Devising from stimuli: textual 16
    Developing your skills 20
Devising from stimuli: visual 21
    Developing use of voice in performance 23
Devising from stimuli: aural 25
    Devising using a verbatim theatre style . 27
    Site specific and promenade theatre ... 28
Devising from stimuli: abstract 29
    Developing character 30
Practicalities: rehearsal and performance 32
Working as a Designer for Component 1: Devising 39
The portfolio 40

Component 2: Performance from Text
Performance from text 46
Component 2: key facts 47
Case study 1: a group performance 49
Case study 2: a duologue or monologue.. 58
Working as a Designer for Component 2: Performance from Text 65

Component 3: Theatre Makers in Practice
Theatre Makers in Practice 66
Component 3: key facts 67
An Inspector Calls 68
The Crucible 77
Government Inspector 88
Twelfth Night 98
DNA 108
1984 117
Blue Stockings 127
Dr Korczak's Example 137
Live Theatre Evaluation 147
    Things to look out for 148
    After the trip 151
    The exam paper 152

Thinking about Working as a Designer?
How does design fit into the GCSE course? 154
What kind of designer should I be? 155
Working as a costume designer 156
Working as a lighting designer 160
Working as a set designer 165
Working as a sound designer 168

Glossary 172

Index 176

The authors

Rhianna Elsden

gained her PGCE in English & Drama in 2002 having graduated from Cambridge University. She has since completed an MEd and an MA. She has worked extensively for Edexcel as an examiner and team leader within Drama & Theatre Studies specifications, and is currently Head of Performing & Creative Arts at a school in Dorset. She is also a Specialist Leader in Education working as a consultant across the Dorset County to improve key areas of the teaching profession. Rhianna is also an award-winning playwright.

Alicia Pope

graduated with a degree in Drama and English from the University of Glamorgan in 1997. After spending some time in India she returned to her home town of Bristol and trained at the University of the West of England to be a teacher. She spent more than ten years teaching drama and was involved in taking student work to the Edinburgh Fringe. Alicia is now a writer, moderator and examiner for A level Theatre Studies and GCSE Drama as well as running a drama club at a local primary school.

David Porter

has enjoyed a varied career. He co-founded and directed Vivid Children's Theatre company in the 1970s, after which he was an English supply teacher in London, then a Head of Drama, followed by sixteen years in politics and then again a high school Head of Drama and Performing Arts. Today he is a writer of teaching materials, and senior A-level and GCSE moderator and assessor. Married with four children and seven grandchildren he lives in East Anglia where he was born and raised. His novel *Old Men's Dreams* was published in 2015 and his autobiography *A Rebel's Journey* is set for publication in 2016.

Lucy Ellen Rix

was a professional Stage Manager in repertory theatre until she trained as a teacher in 2002. She has taught Drama at GCSE, A Level and BTEC in several mainstream secondary schools, and is currently Head of Drama at a specialist school for blind and partially sighted young people where she directs a whole school production each year. Alongside her educational work, Lucy has stage managed for Pendley Shakespeare Festival and directed for Perfect Circle, a youth theatre in Worcestershire.

Sarah Lambie (Series Editor)

graduated with an English degree from Cambridge University in 2007, and went on to train as an actor at the Bristol Old Vic Theatre School. Alongside her performing career, she teaches English, drama and singing, is a freelance arts journalist and the editor of *Teaching Drama* magazine.

Introduction

Congratulations! You have chosen to study a really exciting and rewarding subject for GCSE, and the long-term benefits you'll gain from what you learn are enormous.

Drama is not just for people who want to be performers when they leave school – your time studying this course will equip you with many transferrable life skills: teamwork, listening, public speaking, time management, confidence in your imagination, problem-solving…and as you study your set texts or explore your devising stimuli you will encounter aspects of history, sociology, psychology and many other subjects.

Drama GCSE is not entirely practical: there is a written element to two out of the three components of the course, so although you will spend a good deal of time in a rehearsal studio with your group, you must set aside time to work on these aspects as well – preparing your portfolio and revising for the written exam. There is more on these sections from pages 40 and 66 of this book.

Although this book takes you through all the parts of the GCSE course, your teacher will be your main guide: they will choose your set texts and most likely your devising stimuli, and they will oversee your rehearsal processes. However, throughout all three components, this book will give you ideas which you can apply in your own practical and written work.

How is the course structured?

Your GCSE is divided into three components.

Component 1: Devising accounts for 40% of your GCSE. It is made up of two parts:

1. a practical devised performance worth 15 marks, which you rehearse and present with your group, and
2. a written or recorded portfolio worth 45 marks, which documents and analyses your rehearsal process.

Component 2: Performance from text accounts for 20% of your GCSE. This is also a practical performance, and this time there is no portfolio of evidence to hand in, although you do have to provide 100-200 words summarising your artistic intentions. Rather than devising a piece of theatre you work on two extracts of script from an existing play, and you perform in a small group or alone.

Component 3: Theatre makers in practice accounts for 40% of your GCSE. It is a written exam lasting 1 hour and 30 minutes and is divided into two parts:

1. questions on a set play-text which you will have studied in detail, worth 45 marks, and
2. questions about a live theatre performance you have seen during your GCSE course, worth 15 marks.

How am I marked?

Your final, overall mark for the GCSE will be a grade numbered from 9-1, with 9 being the best available grade.

For each component, your teacher or an external examiner will mark your work according to how well you have met certain 'Assessment Objectives', often shortened to 'AOs'. They will look at how you:

AO1	Create and develop ideas to communicate meaning for theatrical performance
AO2	Apply theatrical skills to realise artistic intentions in live performance
AO3	Demonstrate knowledge and understanding of how drama and theatre is developed and performed
AO4	Analyse and evaluate your own work and the work of others

Not all AOs apply to each component: AO2 cannot be used in component 3, for example, because there is no performance involved. Don't worry, your teacher will ensure that you are working towards meeting these objectives throughout your course.

Do I have to be a good actor to get a high grade in my GCSE?

No! Although drama is often chosen by people who enjoy acting, there are four alternative roles you can choose to take in studying this course, and you don't actually have to get up on stage in front of an audience and perform at all.

You are studying the skills and ideas which go to make up the world of theatre, and you have just as good a chance of the best grades if you choose a **design route** instead of a performing route for your course.

There are four types of designer which you can study to be for the purpose of this course:

- Costume designer
- Lighting designer
- Set designer
- Sound designer

This book gives detailed explanations for what you will be required to do if you choose these routes: there is page dedicated to the design roles at the end of each component's chapter, and a full section on designing from page 154. Design sections of the book are easy to find – the pages are green.

Even if you are not working as a designer in the practical elements, you must understand the roles of performers, directors and designers in order to answer the questions in component 3 – the written exam. People often confuse the duties of directors and designers: a **director** oversees the whole of a production, and works with the actors to develop their performances, while a **designer** is responsible for the way the production looks or sounds, and has nothing to do with the performances given by the actors.

Are there any facts which I should learn?

Unlike GCSE subjects such as history or maths, there aren't very many simple facts for you to revise in drama – instead you are developing skills in performance, design, analysis and evaluation. However, throughout your course, both when you are writing and speaking about your subject, you must use appropriate drama language. Throughout this book, you will find **blue words** like these, which indicate that a full explanation is given in the **glossary** from page 172. It is very important to become familiar with these technical terms and to use them when you are working together and writing your portfolio and exam answers.

Where can I go to do further research?

This book will take you all the way through your course and introduce you to lots of ideas, techniques, theories and skills, but it is a very good idea to research beyond the introductions you'll find here as well. Books in your school or local library will help, and the catalogues of the National Theatre Bookshop and Samuel French theatrical bookshop are both excellent and available online.

The internet is an excellent source of further information, but be sure to double-check your sources, as often you may not know who has written it and how accurate it is.

For links to helpful resources on concepts mentioned in this book, and on the set texts, go to **www.rhinegoldeducation.co.uk** and search for 'Edexcel GCSE Drama Study Guide'.

The Theatre

History of the Theatre

Greek theatre

For thousands of years, Athens was the core of Greek civilisation, and the works of Athenian playwrights are still studied today, including Sophocles, Aeschylus, Aristophanes and Euripides. Writers produced work as part of competitions during festivals dedicated to Dionysus, the god of wine and theatre.

The theatre was called the *theatron* or 'seeing place', with audiences seated in the 'hearing place', the *auditorium*. Audiences could number in excess of 10,000 people so the performances were something for the whole community to attend. The chorus of 12 to 15 people danced and sang in the circular, levelled area called the *orchestra* or 'dancing place'.

Ancient amphitheatres were built for clear acoustics and sightlines. The theatre at Epidavros in Greece is still intact

Masks were an important element of Greek theatre. The exaggerated expression of the masks enabled them to be seen by more of the vast audience and allowed actors to play more than one role. Theatre in ancient Greece was seen as a religious experience, where a moral message was learned and the audience experienced **catharsis**, or cleansing.

WHY DO I NEED TO KNOW THIS?

Ancient Greek theatre has given us many of the things that we see as essential for theatre today. The way the theatre is set out for an audience, the use of scenery, the intense language, and the structure of a tragedy: based on Aristotle's *Poetics*.

Medieval theatre

Medieval theatre used bold characterisations and symbolic versions of events rather than trying to present real life.

The storytelling technique was basic and did not involve detailed plots or complex characters. The main purpose of this heavily church influenced drama was to tell Bible stories: to show religious lessons and inspire morality by encouraging audiences to change their sinful behaviour. Literacy rates were very low so few texts survive from this time.

Death was a common theme in this period. People were faced with death on a daily basis, the dead and dying were not hidden away in hospitals and death was a real, everyday part of life.

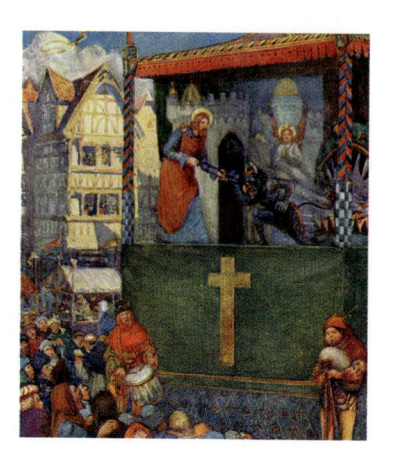

A guild play being performed in the middle ages, circa 14th century

Elizabethan theatre

During the Elizabethan period, education was no longer just for the rich, and more and more people were learning to read and write.

The invention of the printing press some time earlier meant that books and other printed literature were much more widely available and accessible. A focus on the writings of ancient Greek and Roman philosophers and dramatists began to show in the theatre of the time.

THE THEATRE

Elizabethan playwrights moved away from the sequences used in morality plays, and plays became well-structured, reverting to themes of love, power and revenge that were popular in Greek theatre. Plays were character and plot driven, something the audience could really connect with.

During this period James Burbage founded the first permanent playhouse in London, and by 1600 there were a number of dedicated playhouses, mainly on the south bank of the Thames.

The Elizabethan and **Jacobean** periods were the time of Shakespeare, and he and his contemporaries delved into romantic comedies, **satire**, tragedy and revenge tragedy. The Elizabethans loved the theatre in the same way that modern audiences love cinema. Theatre was accessible to everyone, not just the wealthy, and included a cheap standing area in front of the **thrust stage**, occupied by the 'groundlings'.

The original Globe Theatre burnt down in 1613, but it was rebuilt on a site nearby in the 1990s

Restoration Comedy

In 1642 the English civil war began and under the force of the Puritans and Oliver Cromwell, theatres were banned for the next 18 years.

Restoration Comedy refers to the theatre that emerged when King Charles II took the throne and theatre began to return. Theatres were rebuilt, often featuring a **proscenium arch** with a small **apron stage**. Perhaps the biggest innovation was the introduction of female actors: up until now, female roles had been taken on by boys.

Melodrama

Melodrama was popular for most of the 19th century. Melodramas often featured good (often the poor) versus evil (often the wealthy) with **stock characters** or stereotypes that were easily identified by the audience.

There was often lots of music and a fast paced, action packed plot. Audience sizes grew and this required larger theatres: with this increase in size came a loss of subtlety in acting which helped to develop the exaggerated style that we associate with melodrama.

The role of the villain, popular in melodrama, is a character we easily recognise in many modern forms of entertainment, from books and comics to film and television.

Naturalism

Towards the end of the 19th century, **naturalism** became the dominant form in European theatre. Naturalism was intended to show real life on stage with a definite beginning, middle and end and modern, relevant characters.

A key feature of naturalism was the **fourth wall** which could not be broken. A central figure of this period was Konstantin Stanislavski who developed a 'system' by which he trained actors not just to play a character on stage but to 'be' that character.

WHY DO I NEED TO KNOW THIS?

A naturalistic style is often how we choose to portray a story on stage. We want the audience to feel like they are watching real life unfold. We see this convention in many of our favourite television shows, especially soap operas.

Theatre Layouts

Not all theatres or acting spaces are laid out in the same way. When creating your own performance pieces for assessment you may choose a staging depending on your chosen text or theme.

Proscenium arch

This is what we think of as a typical theatre space with a stage at one end and the audience seated in rows facing it.

Originally from ancient Greek theatre, the **proscenium** (meaning 'in front of the scenery') refers to the arch or window that surrounds the stage. This means that the audience are all getting the same view as each other:

Anything that is not in the window becomes backstage, giving us the **wings** at the sides of the stage. The imaginary wall between the actors and the audience at the front of the stage is often referred to as the **fourth wall**. If an actor steps across this, or talks directly to the audience then he is described as 'breaking the fourth wall'.

The restored Loews Theatre in Journal Square, Jersey City, New Jersey

Positives:
- The only danger in actors' positioning is 'upstaging', but it's otherwise easy to avoid having your back to the audience
- The wings allow for **properties (props)** to be stored out of sight until needed
- There are lots of opportunities for using scenery

Negatives:
- Some audiences can feel too distanced from the acting
- There's often a big gap between actors and audience so actors must be good at using their voices

Theatre in the round

This is when the audience are seated on all four sides of the stage. **Theatre in the round** can involve a stage of any shape as long as the audience are on all sides.

The Stephen Joseph Theatre in Scarborough is a good example of this kind of space, but the same impact can be created in a drama studio by placing your audience seating in a large circle or square, with the actors in the centre.

Inside the Stephen Joseph Theatre

Positives:
- Plays can feel very intimate when staged in the round as the audience feel very much part of the action
- There can be lots of freedom with entrances and exits as directors can choose to have actors enter through the audience

Negatives:
- You can't use much scenery
- Blocking (deciding on actors movements) can be difficult to manage because actors are bound to have their backs to the audience at some point

Traverse

Occasionally known as alley, corridor or sandwich theatre (think of the stage as your sandwich filling); **traverse** is when the audience are seated on two sides opposite each other with the stage in the middle.

This kind of staging is often used for fashion shows as well as for theatre.

Positives:
- As with theatre in the round, this kind of staging can be very intimate and allows the actors to interact with the audience
- The audience are more aware of each other during the performance which can make for a more enjoyable experience, or can create tension if required

Negatives:
- Lighting can be difficult as lights will throw shadows onto the actors' faces when seen from the opposite side
- Blocking can be complicated to make sure that actors can be seen by both sides of the audience

Thrust

A **thrust stage** is the oldest kind of staging as it comes from the ancient Greek and Roman arenas.

A thrust stage extends out beyond the proscenium arch into the audience, who surround it on three sides. Like the proscenium arch it still has a backstage area but not wing space. The Globe Theatre is an excellent example of a thrust stage.

The thrust stage at the Globe Theatre, London

Positives:
- This kind of staging provides more intimacy than the proscenium arch
- It provides a good, all round view of the action

Negatives:
- There is only space for large scenery at the back of the stage (upstage)
- Some large props could block the view for audience members so designers need to choose with caution

Promenade

This type of staging is when the audience are required to follow the actors around during the performance.

Promenade staging is often used during outdoor theatre. These types of performances are also sometimes **site specific** if they are designed for a particular location such as a stately home or gardens.

Positives:
- There is often no need for regular seating as the audience can stand or sit while watching and locations will often change for different scenes
- The actors are able to interact a lot with the audience as they are sharing the same space

Negatives:
- It can be very difficult to rehearse this type of theatre as it can be unpredictable
- Actors need to be very skilled to be in control of moving the audience on from one place to another
- There's not much opportunity for props or scenery

Component 1

Devising

This component offers the challenge of working collaboratively with others to explore a range of stimuli in order to create an original performance piece.

You will develop skills in group work, research and negotiation, while also developing your creativity, performance and design skills.

You will consider the impact you can have on an audience and develop ideas you want to communicate.

What does devising mean in drama?

Solitary scribbling by a writer to develop a script that is then passed on for interpretation by directors and actors isn't the only way to create theatre.

Devising is a process in which the whole creative team develops a show collaboratively. Actors, designers, technicians – all can be involved in the creative process. It is an exciting way to produce original material for an audience.

The history of devised theatre

When exactly devised theatre began is impossible to pinpoint; in some cultures, actors being the creators of their work has always been the working method.

It was in the 1960's that the practice seemed to gather momentum, or at least, to become more 'mainstream' and 'credited' in the UK. A number of theatre practitioners at this time started experimenting and making a point of the actor being a creative artist in their own right, as opposed to a worker serving to carry out the wishes of the writer and director. At the same time, many companies started experimenting with radical interpretations of existing play texts, incorporating new devised material. In 1963 one of the first fully devised performances, *Oh, What a Lovely War!* was created by Joan Littlewood and the Theatre Workshop, to critical acclaim.

Today, theatre companies such as Cornwall-based Kneehigh work in the 'devised theatre' form to produce highly praised and commercially successful performances. Each devising theatre company puts their work together in very different ways, and the work that comes out of their own idiosyncratic process is equally varied and unique. The same will be true for you as you seek to form your original piece with your group.

Oh, What a Lovely War! performed in June 1965

COMPONENT 1: DEVISING

Component 1: key facts

This component accounts for 40% of your GCSE and is worth 60 marks.

You can work as a performer or a designer for this component to:
- Create and develop a devised piece from a stimulus
- Perform this devised piece or realise the design of the piece
- Analyse and evaluate the devising process and performance in an accompanying portfolio

This component is internally assessed by your teacher and then externally moderated by the exam board.

There are two parts to the assessment. These are the bits which will be marked:

1. **a portfolio** analysing and evaluating the process leading to the development of the original piece. This is worth 45 marks.
2. the performance of a **devised piece** for those taking the performance route OR **a design realisation** in performance for those opting to take the design route; both must be recorded as evidence by your school or college. This is worth 15 marks.

> An outline of what the portfolio should contain and how it can be recorded and submitted can be found on pages 40-45 of this book.

WHY DO I NEED TO KNOW THIS?
It is important to remember that a great final performance or design realisation without the accompanying portfolio will not see you pass this component. You may enjoy working on the piece as a performer or designer most of all, but remember that **the portfolio is worth 45 marks and the performance only 15.**

Group sizes and time limits

A group must contain between 3 and 6 performance students. In addition, there can be up to one designer per role, per group. Roles available for design are:

- Costume design
- Lighting design
- Set design
- Sound design

> If you are planning to be a designer in this component, turn to page 39 to see what you will be required to do, and then look at pages 154-171 for tips on each role.

Though you work in a group, you are assessed as an individual.
There is no set time for how long you have to put the work together. This will be something your teacher plans. You must, though, perform within the following time limits:

Group size	Timings
3-4 performance students	Between 10-15 minutes
5-6 performance students	Between 20-25 minutes

Choice of stimuli

Your original devised piece can be developed from any stimulus. Your teacher will give you something to start generating ideas from.

Stimuli could be one or a combination of:
- Textual e.g. a novel, poem, story, letter, factual material
- Visual e.g. a painting, photograph, film or artefact
- Aural e.g. a piece of music, a soundscape or a recording
- Abstract e.g. a word, a theme or a mood

As well as selecting the stimulus, you must be able to demonstrate how you have used it to create and develop a performance piece. This will be in your portfolio.

Though you work in a group, you must keep a record of your own individual contribution throughout. It is better to do this all the way through the process rather than trying to remember things at the end.

How do we devise from the stimuli?

Your teacher may have very set structures for each lesson, or you may be given a very loose structure on how to work with the stimuli you have chosen or been given.

The next few pages will outline some of the choices for stimuli and ways in which you might choose to develop the performance. There is, however, no right or wrong.

You will find the openness of devising and having nothing set in stone both liberating and terrifying at different stages of the process. You will get stuck sometimes. The key is to communicate with your group and seek ways forward together and with support from your teacher.

Don't sit back and wait for others to come up with ideas, if you do – you'll have nothing to write about for the portfolio and you might not be happy with the role you are given in the performance. If you do suggest an idea and it isn't used, don't take it personally, as not everything can be in the final performance. If you have lots of ideas, don't dominate the group; resentment will quickly build if someone doesn't listen or take into account the ideas and feelings of others.

COMPONENT 1: DEVISING

Creating aims for your devised work

Knowing the aims and intentions for your piece will help you to keep momentum.

It will also help you to decide whether what you are developing is appropriate and worth pursuing, because if it doesn't serve your aims, then it isn't. Deciding on aims and objectives will also help you when you evaluate the piece, which is part of the portfolio requirement.

> **SOME THINGS TO CONSIDER:**
> - Who are we making this piece for? Who will our audience be?
> - What do we want the audience to get from our work – e.g. do we want to make them laugh, to educate them, to shock them?
> - What is inspiring in the stimulus material for us?
> - What style or structure might we go for?
> - Is what we have in mind practical?
> - What extra research might we need to do?
> - Where will we perform the piece and will this have an influence on what we produce?
> - Do we want our audience to be passive observers, or involved in some way?

You might like to have a mind-map in your portfolio of your aims, intentions and objectives for the piece.

Inspiring companies

You shouldn't try to copy others – this is original work – but some of the working methods and styles of the theatre companies listed below, who largely use devising as their method for creating work, could help to inspire you.

Many of them have highly visual, slick websites with pictures, trailers, blogs and so on, which could inspire your group. It could also just provide some welcome relief to watch and read about someone else's affirmation that devising is a wonderful way to create exciting theatre, when you are working through the challenges yourself:

- Kneehigh
- Frantic Assembly
- DV8
- Punchdrunk
- Stan's Café
- Tangled Feet
- Gecko Theatre Company

You will be able to find more inspiration too, by typing 'devised theatre' into a search engine, but note that some of the work produced by the companies is not suitable for those under 16.

Frantic Assembly's production of *Othello*, 2014

Devising from stimuli: textual

The textual stimuli could be in the form of such things as a novel, poem, story, letter or factual material. You will be given a stimulus by your teacher at the beginning of the process.

In the next few pages are some examples of what you might get as a starting point and things you might do in working from the stimulus. The methods for exploration, though, are not specific to the stimuli – you can mix and match.

Remember, your teacher may give suggestions on how you work and develop material, but ultimately the decisions are yours. Always try to get up on your feet and work practically as early as possible: it's easy to get caught up in discussion, but you're here to devise.

Textual stimuli: poetry

Imagine you are to use the following poem by Roger McGough as a stimulus:

```
A millionbillionwillion miles from home
Waiting for the bell to go. (To go where?)
Why are they all so big, other children?
So noisy? So much at home they
Must have been born in uniform
Lived all their lives in playgrounds
Spent the years inventing games
That don't let me in. Games
That are rough, that swallow you up.

And the railings.
All around, the railings.
Are they to keep out wolves and monsters?
Things that carry off and eat children?
Things you don't take sweets from?
Perhaps they're to stop us getting out
Running away from the lessins. Lessin.
What does a lessin look like?
Sounds small and slimy.
They keep them in the glassrooms.
Whole rooms made out of glass. Imagine.

I wish I could remember my name
Mummy said it would come in useful.
Like wellies. When there's puddles.
Yellowwellies. I wish she was here.
I think my name is sewn on somewhere
Perhaps the teacher will read it for me.
Tea-cher. The one who makes the tea.
```

COMPONENT 1: DEVISING

Having read the poem, some potential next steps could be:

As a group, discuss the poem:
- What do you/don't you like about it?
- Are there any words you don't understand?
- How does it make you feel?
- What pictures does it create in your mind?
- Can you relate to it?
- What is it about?
- Is there a plot?
- How old do you think the poem is? How can you tell?

Don't forget – you need to put in your portfolio your reactions to the stimulus and how you worked from it, so keep making notes, either in the lesson, or immediately afterwards.

> **Pages 40-45 of this book give you advice on how to build a good portfolio.**

Research

You could do some research to find out more about the writer and the poem.
You might find other poems by the writer that you want to link into the work you are developing. Your research might lead you to find out interesting things about the writer which you decide to pursue for your piece. Or you might decide that you want to explore themes rather than the writer. This could develop into looking at first days at school, or something else to do with education.

Do I have to do extra research?

There should be some evidence in your work and portfolio that you have done research on or inspired by the stimulus. Not only is this required, it's something that will prove useful – you never know where it could lead the work. It is unlikely that on its own the stimulus will be enough to fill or shape the entire performance.

Where relevant, you should research:
- Social, historical and cultural **contexts**
- Theatrical conventions
- Current themes and trends
- Issues and controversies

> **In the coming pages, look out for ideas as to how you can incorporate these key terms into your devising work.**

Practical exploration: tableaux/still images

You could turn the poem stimulus into a series of still images. This would help you to explore the narrative. You can also take photos of this exploration to use in your portfolio. If they are in your portfolio, annotate around the images in text boxes drawing attention to the key features and using drama language.

GCSE DRAMA STUDY GUIDE

When creating a **tableau** or still image, you need to consider things like:

- **Proxemics**
- Use of space
- Facial expressions
- Levels
- Eye contact
- Posture
- Body language
- Gesture

Who knows – this exploration could produce images that are included in the final devised piece…

What could we do next?

The options are endless – that's the exciting thing about devising.

You could move into some **hot seating** now to create the central character in the poem. Hot seating is where you have someone in role as a character responding to questions from another student, or the group. This helps develop depth to a role and because answers are not always planned, the improvised responses can lead into unexpected and rich ideas. For this reason, it's worth recording hot seating, or having someone take notes.

You could develop a **movement sequence** with one person narrating and everyone else acting out the poem.

Unexpected spiralling of ideas

The poem might seem to be leading you to produce a naturalistic play about school. It might seem, so far, to be quite light-hearted as a developing piece. This could be the way your work develops and you could decide that an aim is to make your audience laugh and reflect on their own time in school.

However, there is nothing to stop you taking a much more serious path inspired by the poem. You might decide that the poem will not directly feature at all in your final piece. Instead, you might choose to look at education around the world today and some children's fight to be educated. This could lead you to explore Malala Yousafzai's inspiring story, for example.

Malala is a Pakistani activist for female education and the youngest-ever Nobel Prize laureate. In 2012 she was shot by the Taliban in her native Swat Valley in northwest Pakistan while on her way to school. The Taliban had destroyed many schools in the area and had banned girls from attending those still open. Malala had been defiantly creating a blog to let the world know about the restriction on her right to education; after she was shot the world helped her in what became a fight for her life, not just for education. There is lots on her and her story online. Even though the poem might have been seemingly sending you on a less socially/culturally topical path, you could send it in this direction, for example.

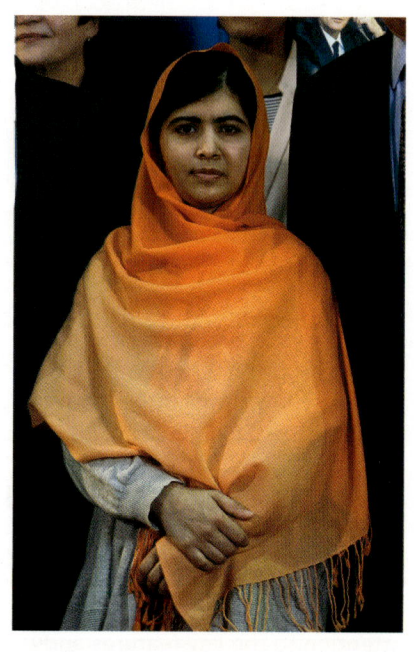

Malala Yousafzai in 2014

COMPONENT 1: DEVISING

Textual stimuli: factual information

Imagine this was your stimulus – an article from a newspaper:

How much hidden sugar is in YOUR diet?

Study reveals that a bowl of tomato soup or natural yogurt has as much sugar as a bowl of Frosties

- Leading professor has compiled a list of everyday 'hidden sugar' offenders
- These include flavoured water, yogurts, canned soup, ready meals and bread
- Graham MacGregor says food industry is adding more sugar to food
- Says many people fall for the 'low fat' trick – not realising food is packed with sugar instead to give it flavour

We are constantly told how much sugar there is in fizzy drinks and cakes. But what about the hidden sugar in so-called healthy foods?

A leading professor has spoken out about the dangers of 'hidden sugar' in food.

He also cautions against opting for low fat foods that are often full of sugar instead to give them flavour.

Graham MacGregor, Professor of Cardiovascular Medicine at the Wolfson Institute of Preventive Medicine at Barts and The London Hospital, says the food industry is adding more and more sugar to food, which consumers are largely unaware of, as it is mostly hidden….

Again, you might begin by discussing the article, or going online to research the rest of it and related articles. There is lots of potential here to connect with current themes and trends and as an aim for the piece you could potentially seek to educate your audience in some way on health and diet.

Why not approach this from an unexpected angle?

- Using **physical theatre**, how could you show 'hidden sugar'?
- Could you create a **naturalistic** scene in which everyone is having breakfast and then it turns into an advert to warn of the dangers of hidden sugar in products?
- Maybe you could **improvise** a situation where Professor Graham MacGregor decides to talk to someone at random in a bus queue who likes fizzy drinks?

GCSE DRAMA STUDY GUIDE

DEVELOPING YOUR SKILLS

If you are intending to be marked as a performer in the piece you are putting together, as you work you are expected to develop skills in:

- Rehearsing and learning lines: adapting work in response to rehearsals (to be done collaboratively)
- Voice: use of clarity, pace, **inflection**, pitch and **projection**
- Physicality: the use of space, gesture, stillness and stance
- Ability to combine and apply vocal skills
- Characterisation
- Communication with other performers and with the audience
- Understanding of style, **genre** and theatrical conventions

Designers are expected to develop skills in:

- Making appropriate judgements during the development process
- Creating clear and practical designs (e.g. creating plans/plots/diagrams/sketches) with consideration into practical application of materials and production elements
- Adapting designs in response to rehearsals (to be done collaboratively)
- Using visual/aural elements to create mood, atmosphere and style
- Using, applying and combining design skills to contribute to and support the performance as a whole
- Demonstrating the ability to apply design skills effectively within the context of the performance
- Communicating intention and creating impact for an audience

What are 'theatrical conventions'?

There is a range of theatrical conventions (techniques) that have been used to create dramatic effects in plays for centuries. Among these are:

- slow motion
- **tableaux**
- audience **aside**
- **split focus**
- flashback/flash-forward
- narration
- spoken thought
- **soliloquy**

What is meant by 'style of the performance'?

Style indicates a specific way of performing. Sometimes a style is linked closely with a particular practitioner e.g. **naturalism** is associated with the Russian practitioner Stanislavski; **physical theatre** is linked with Artaud, or more recently, with Frantic Assembly, for example.

Other styles and genres you could pick for your work could be:

- Comedy
- Tragedy
- Melodrama
- Musical Theatre
- Theatre in Education

Your task is to show your teacher that you understand these and how they have influenced your preparation and final performance.

COMPONENT 1: DEVISING

Devising from stimuli: visual

Visual stimuli could take the form of a painting, photograph, film or artefact.

Imagine you are given the photograph above as your stimulus or starting point:

Things it might inspire you to consider:

- What can you see?
- Where/when was it taken?
- Is it real?
- Is there a plot/narrative to the image?
- Does it have a message?
- What could be a title for the image?
- Can you relate to it?
- What happened before the photo was taken/what will happen next?
- Do you like it? Justify your response.

Developing work inspired by the image

Again, you could undertake some research. It seems to connect to the issues and potential controversies within global warming, for example, which could then be at the centre of your piece.

Soundscape

As a way of working with the image, you could create a **soundscape** with your group.

When creating a soundscape, you can either improvise it, or structure it to work out what noises will come in at which moments. You could choose to have one member of the group as a conductor, while the rest of the group are the 'orchestra'. Using their voices the group paints a soundscape linked to a place, mood, theme or in this case, a picture. The leader can control the shape of the piece by raising or lowering their hand to increase or decrease the volume. You may also use simple percussion instruments or objects around you in the space.

This initially improvised sequence could be something a design candidate working on music or sound uses to inspire them. You could record the actors and manipulate the sounds using computer music packages, or create a brand new more 'realistic' soundscape using computer packages and pre-recorded sound effects.

It could be that the sounds are played through different speakers around the audience to create a surround experience that really puts them in the middle of the environment. Panning – where you choose which speakers the music comes through – is something that many sound desks and computer packages are able to manipulate.

Using music or sound while devising, or as a stimulus, and not just for the final performance is something done by many theatre companies in their devising processes and in their final devised work.

THEATRE COMPANY INSPIRATION: FRANTIC ASSEMBLY

'Music is a massive inspiration to us. We have it in our heads all the time and we use it in rehearsals at every stage. We cannot understand the type of rehearsal where the music only arrives in the tech week. It is integral to how we understand and communicate our theatre. It is a very present collaborator throughout the rehearsal process.

The important thing is that you find and use the music that inspires you and your group to be creative and that gives the atmosphere you'd like to create in your sessions.'

You can find more on how Frantic Assembly create theatre by going to their website: www.franticassembly.co.uk and looking at their downloads and resource packs.

Ignition, Frantic Assembly, 2015

COMPONENT 1: DEVISING

DEVELOPING USE OF VOICE IN PERFORMANCE

One of the areas performers are marked on for this component is the use of voice. You are expected to demonstrate control over clarity, pace, inflection, pitch and projection.

As you go through the rehearsal process, guide each other in the group to reflect on the progress each of you is making.

Clarity: Are all your consonants and vowels clearly defined?

Pace: Are you able to speed up and slow down your delivery when the scene and the character's emotional circumstances demand it?

Inflection: Are you making the right alterations in your tone to communicate meaning?

Pitch: How high or low does your voice need to be at each point that you're speaking?

Projection: Are you reaching the back of the audience with a properly supported voice?

Developing breath control

Breathing is something we do unconsciously and we take for granted. In acting though, if you're not in control of your breathing during a long speech, you could suddenly run out of breath, ruining the delivery.

It is a common belief that we breathe with our lungs alone, when actually the whole body does the work of breathing. Understanding how you personally breathe is important because 'everyday breathing' and 'actor breathing' are different, and you will need to develop your breath control as an actor.

- Start by standing up straight in front of a long mirror.
- Be aware of your posture – the way you stand will affect your breath. If you're slouching, you're shortening your lung capacity.
- Pay attention to your breath as you inhale and exhale. What happens to your body? Are there any places you hold tension? Are you breathing from your diaphragm or your chest? Your aim is to use the **diaphragm** as this maximises the amount of air in your lungs.
- As you breathe in, watch your shoulders. They should stay in place and not rise.
- Put your hands on your sides, over your rib cage – you should feel them move outwards and inwards.

Once you are aware of how you breathe and the things you are doing that are shortening your breath, you can then become more skilled at controlling things like posture and your use of your diaphragm. Books and online resources, including videos, are available to help, should you want to learn more.

In rehearsals, and ahead of the final performance, include exercises and warm-ups for your vocal muscles and indeed your whole body. Including time for exercises and games linked to developing vocality, physicality and characterisation can also help break up some potential staleness that might creep in to rehearsals.

For more tips on rehearsing, turn to page 32.

DEVELOPING PROJECTION

Naturally, the audience needs to hear what you are saying, therefore projecting your voice is very important. Again, the way we project our voices in everyday speech is something we don't often think about.

As an actor, you do though have to be more aware of projection and, as with breath control, it involves the whole body. If you simply rely on pushing your vocal chords to make your voice heard, you will soon lose your voice.

- Centre your body, releasing tension and standing with equal weight on each foot.
- Pick a line that you say in performance – speak it at your normal volume.
- Be aware of your body as you speak – you are aiming to remain relaxed and loose.
- Now pick a point across the room and say the line again as if you are trying to make your volume reach that point.
- Don't tense up – be especially aware of raising your shoulders or tilting your head back which will tighten your neck muscles, putting strain on your vocal chords.
- Now increase the challenge by picking a point further away and aim to project your voice to that distance.
- Increasing your volume during a warm-up should be done a stage at a time. If you suddenly go from quiet to loud this will not develop your ability, it will damage your vocal chords. They need to be stretched at intervals to reach the louder level that you need for performance.

The Alexander technique

Named after Frederick Matthias Alexander, this technique teaches people how to avoid unnecessary muscular and mental tension during their everyday activities. He developed it in the 1890s because he was suffering from a loss of voice when performing. Alexander realised that he had been holding tension in his neck, and indeed his whole body, which was causing him to lose his voice while acting.

Frederick Matthias Alexander

The purpose of the Alexander technique is to help people unlearn bad physical habits they don't even realise they have and return to a balanced state in which the body is well aligned. Seek out his exercises in books or online to learn more for yourself.

In addition to breath control and projection, you could complete exercises to help with articulation (such as tongue-twisters), and facial exercises to warm up the jaw and tongue.

COMPONENT 1: DEVISING

Devising from stimuli: aural

Aural stimuli could take the form of a piece of music, a soundscape or a recording.

As a stimulus, imagine you have been played a song with the following lyrics:

This city never sleeps
I hear the people walk by when
   it's late
Sirens bleed through my
   windowsill
I can't close my eyes
Don't control what I'm into
This tower is alive
The lights that blind keep me
   awake
With my hood up and lace untied
Sleep fills my mind
Don't control what I'm into

London calls me a stranger
A traveller
This is now my home, my home
I'm burning on the back street
Stuck here sitting in the
   backseat
I'm blazing on the street
What I do isn't up to you
And if the city never sleeps
Then that makes two

The pavement is my friend
Hey, and it will take me where
   I need to go
I find it trips me up
And puts me down
This is not what I'm used to
The shop across the road
Fulfils my needs and gives me
   company

When I need it
Voices speak through my walls
I don't think I'm gonna make it
Past tomorrow

London calls me a stranger
A traveller
This is now my home, my home
I'm burning on the back street
Stuck here sitting in the
   backseat
I'm blazing on the street
What I do isn't up to you
And if the city never sleeps
Then that makes two

And my lungs hurt
And my ears bled
With the sound of the city life
Echoed in my head
Do I need this to keep me alive?
The traffic stops and starts
But I need to move along

London calls me a stranger
This is not my home
I'm burning on the back street
Stuck here sitting in the
   backseat
I'm blazing on the street
What I do isn't up to you
And if the city never sleeps
Then that makes two

Developing work inspired by the lyrics

This song, *The City* by Ed Sheeran, could lead you to take a thematic turn in the development of your work. You might decide that this stimulus leads you into exploring London as a theme, as this is mentioned several times in the lyrics. There seems to be discussion of being homeless in a big city in the lyrics as well, which could also inspire your work to follow this issue.

Improvisation

Your group could set up an environment and place a person centrally in role as 'the homeless person'. They have to improvise as a series of people (the rest of the group) pass by with their improvised different reactions or non-reactions to the homeless character.

Cross-cutting

Sometimes a drama that starts and carries on in a linear manner can be too predictable, which could make it boring to watch. With **cross-cutting** you could show the moment when something important happened in the past (using a **flash-back**), or you could move the drama forward in time (using a **flash-forward**). In this way the action can be broken up to enhance **tension** or the narrative. You can show back-story this way. You could even have two scenes on stage side-by-side at the same time to show the 'before' and 'after'.

With this stimulus, you could develop a scene showing the character homeless and walking the streets of London now, and then cross-cut back in time to show us what led to this situation.

You could develop a **monologue** by the homeless character which could go anywhere in the structure because if it is non-linear then the ordering of scenes is up to you and your group.

If you do develop a monologue, this could be done just from your group's imagination, or maybe after some **hot seating**.

Alternatively, you might decide to do research into being homeless, and find some testimonies by homeless people that are very useful for creating a monologue and building the piece or characters.

If you use direct testimonies by other people, then you are devising using the **verbatim theatre** style.

COMPONENT 1: DEVISING

Devising using a verbatim theatre style

Verbatim theatre is a form of documentary theatre that employs (largely or exclusively) tape-recorded material from the real lives of people interviewed to give it its dramatic shape. In so doing, it is theatre that claims a degree of authority and 'truth'.

The 1963 devised play *Oh, What a Lovely War!* was formed using some verbatim methods, knitting together actual soldier diary entries and researched material found by the cast.

The Laramie Project (2000) by Moisés Kaufman and members of the Tectonic Theatre Project, about the reaction to the 1998 murder of gay student Matthew Shepard in Laramie, Wyoming, is another highly regarded example. The play draws on hundreds of interviews conducted by the theatre company with inhabitants of the town, company members' own journal entries, and published news reports. Using verbatim testimonies is highly popular today as a way of developing material for theatrical performance.

Playwright Mark Wheeller mixes verbatim material with his own ideas to put his original work together. *Too Much Punch for Judy* and *Hard to Swallow* are key examples; reading Wheeller's work you might find that the way he structures his plays and the way he uses narration is useful for your own work. Go to **newwheellerplays.co.uk**.

Creating work in this way can make it highly relevant to you or perhaps to your local area, and could have a big impact on your chosen audience.

Programme cover from the original production of Oh, What A Lovely War! *at the Theatre Royal Stratford East in March 1963*

Actor/audience relationship

One of the requirements of your performance is that you will have aims for how you want your audience to respond. You will have objectives in mind for what they will get out of the experience. You have to evaluate how well this has been achieved as part of your portfolio.

The relationship between the work, the cast and your audience is the most important aspect of any devised work.

Another of the things you might need to consider is the placement of the audience and whether you want to involve them in any way, or whether you are keeping 'traditional' boundaries between audience and performance space.

> Pages 10–11 of this book contain some ideas for theatre layouts and their potential positives and negatives. You might be very restricted in your choices due to the restraints of the room you have to perform in, but even in the most limited of spaces, you need to think about how you are going to establish an actor/audience relationship.

Site-specific theatre

In considering the actor-audience relationship, you might choose a **site-specific** theatre style whereby you use the properties, qualities and meanings of the space to inform the work created. This can form a very powerful link between the work, the actor and the audience. Sometimes the space has stories linked to its history that could lead into exciting and original work.

Researching online some site-specific theatre companies who work in this way can be inspiring. Some names you might like to look up are:

- Talking Birds theatre company
- Kabosh theatre company
- Grid Iron theatre company

If you decide you like this style, it could mean you pick a different place within your school site in which to perform, or indeed pick a completely new place, away from your school. If you do, always check for permissions as the space may be restricted for performances for some reason.

Promenade theatre

Another interesting way of establishing or experimenting with the actor/audience relationship is by using a **promenade theatre** style.

In promenade theatre, the audience moves among the action that takes place within a defined space. It is a style that demands commitment from the audience and inventive ways by the actor to direct the audience's attention towards where the next scene is going to take place. You could devise a site-specific promenade piece from your stimuli and again it might not even be set within your school grounds.

> **ATTENTION:** It is essential that a good recording of your performance is made for moderation – therefore your teacher must be positive that this can be achieved before you decide to devise a site-specific or promenade performance.

THEATRE COMPANY INSPIRATION: PUNCHDRUNK

Punchdrunk are a British theatre company established in 2000 who take the idea of promenade and site-specific theatre even further, offering a style of immersive theatre in which the audience are not directed around the space, but fully interact and play a part within the performance.

'Punchdrunk was born through a desire to create theatrical work in which the audience is at the centre of the experience. We strive to wrench them from the safety and passivity of traditional theatre seats and place them at the heart of the action, equipped with identity and purpose.

Immersive theatre enables you to be physically present, and experiences become fuelled by adrenalin and curiosity. This added dimension of tactility brings a frisson of danger to the adventure, making you more sensorially aware and engaged with the base physical responses from your body. From entry into the space right through to the exit at the end of the night, we want each element of a Punchdrunk show to be stimulating and all consuming for audiences, enabling them to become completely lost in the worlds we create.'

Felix Barrett, artistic director of Punchdrunk.

COMPONENT 1: DEVISING

Devising from stimuli: abstract

Abstract stimuli could be a word, a theme or a mood.

Imagine you have been given just this word as your abstract stimulus:

Refugee

Once again, you might begin your exploration with research.

You might choose to have a group or class discussion on what the word means to you or makes you think about.

You could form a **tableau** or **still image** connected to the word as an instant practical response.

Forum Theatre

You could use forum theatre to explore the word, or indeed any stimulus.

Firstly you might develop a scene in which someone is trying to cross a country's border as a refugee. You might do some research to give this some depth in terms of a location, or a reason that the person might be fleeing their own country. The scene plays out to another group within your class. Those watching are encouraged to stop the action when they think it necessary, to suggest a different way the action could develop. At other times, you as the actors might stop the action, and ask for help. The audience can be given permission to step in and take over a role – or even introduce a new one – should they wish to do so. You can rewind and re-try action with the new suggestions added in.

This technique can be useful because it might be hard, when devising drama, to imagine what a person might do or say at a particular moment. It could help develop narrative or indeed character. You could use the developed scene directly in the work, or ideas generated from it and the input from others watching.

Augusto Boal

Forum Theatre was developed by Brazilian theatre practitioner Augusto Boal. He would actually have it as a performance technique rather than a way of devising material. In his model, the 'spect-actor' – any member of the audience – would know that coming to the performance would mean they were encouraged to be active and stop the action to offer suggestions. For Boal he saw it as a way to address political issues and connect performers and audience equally. It enabled participants to try out courses of action which could be applicable to their everyday lives.

Augusto Boal works with students in New York City, May 2008

THEATRE COMPANY INSPIRATION: CARDBOARD CITIZENS

Cardboard Citizens is the UK's only homeless people's professional theatre company and the leading practitioner of forum theatre in the UK. Founded in 1991, they work with people who have experience of, or who are at risk of, becoming homeless. They cite Augusto Boal as their inspiration, and their founder, Adrian Jackson, translated a number of his books.

Cardboard Citizens' website outlines more of their work and how they link to Augusto Boal and his Theatre of the Oppressed. It also outlines more about the way forum theatre can be used: www.cardboardcitizens.org.uk

DEVELOPING CHARACTER: ROLE ON THE WALL

During the development of your piece, to increase the depth of a character you could try creating a role on the wall.

For this, the outline of a body is drawn on a sheet of paper. Words or phrases describing the character are then written directly onto the drawing or stuck on with post-its. This can be carried out as a group activity or by individuals writing about their own character. You can include known facts such as physical appearance, gender, age and occupation, as well as subjective ideas such as likes, dislikes, motivations, secrets and aspirations.

You can choose to have known facts written around the outline, and thoughts and feelings inside. You can return to add more ideas, thoughts and feelings as you discover more about the character over time. You can do this for fictional or non-fictional characters.

Developing character: Stanislavski's system

Konstantin Stanislavski was originally an actor and then a director. Though he died in 1938, his ideas on acting technique and developing characters in theatre are still used and discussed today.

Stanislavski treated theatre-making as a serious endeavour requiring dedication and discipline. Throughout his life, he subjected his own acting to a process of intense self-analysis and reflection. His 'system' aimed to help an actor achieve an 'artistic truth' on stage where performances were totally believable to the audience.

He is usually associated with scripted performance, but some of his techniques could be applied to devised work, especially once the overall structure of the piece has been developed.

Given circumstances

The given circumstances are usually the character details in the script – the facts the playwright gives the actor about the character's life and surroundings.

For devised work, these are still useful things to decide, and then consider the effect that these 'truths' might have on the person and how you play them.

Questions to ask might include:

- Where am I?
- What year is it?
- What relationships do I have?
- What has happened before the play begins?
- Have I any past experiences which may affect the way I react to events in the play?

COMPONENT 1: DEVISING

your performance it will be useful to keep the idea of objectives in mind. What is your character trying to achieve, what do they want? Tensions arise in any human story when characters differ in what they want; and tension usually makes for good drama.

Emotional memory

In Stanislavski's system, the actor does not 'act' emotions or states such as sad, happy, or mad. Instead, using **emotional memory**, you remember a situation in which you felt the same, or similar, emotions as your character. Recalling the situation leads to emotion.

Units and objectives

Stanislavski would break a play down into units with objectives.

A unit of a scene is a section which contains a single aim or objective for the actor: what are you trying to do to, or get from the other characters in the scene with you? When your objective, or aim, changes because of the progression of the scene or the dialogue, the unit changes too. When devising the script for

This exercise can be damaging if not treated with care – it is important that the actor doesn't force a memory, or bring up something hurtful. It can be just as useful to remember a relatively minor negative emotion from your life and then imagine it heightened to the extent felt by the character: this will ensure that you feel rather than act the emotion in the play, but don't allow your work to affect your real life. It is a play, and the word 'play' is associated with fun for good reasons.

> **To find out more about the system and other practical activities for developing depth within your acting, look online or read Stanislavski's books.**

As can be seen in the past pages, what you will be given as a starting point could be literally anything. There are no restrictions by the exam board and it is up to your teacher to choose what will work best for your group to begin developing your work from.

Similarly, the way you then work from the stimulus can take many paths. You can be inspired to work in ways suggested by past theatre practitioners, current theatre companies or well-known drama devising techniques. Or you could choose none of these and create your own devising route. This is what makes devised theatre so exciting, and also scary – the page is blank – there's nothing to perform, or for an audience to watch, until you create it!

Practicalities: rehearsal and performance

Scheduling

Though devising can be unpredictable and must be open enough to allow experimentation and exploration, there must be an end product for the audience.

In your case, the end product is examined and everything you do and plan has to serve the objective of getting the performance completed to the highest standard, in time.

Creating a schedule could help you with organisation. Start by putting down your end performance date and then work backwards. Here is an example of how you might structure a production schedule. It would need to be formed by everyone in your group and for all to have a copy so that you can ensure everyone is working towards the same timescales.

Insert date	Begin working on performance in class
Insert date	**Aims & basic structure of final performance to be in place**
Insert date	Development and rehearsals
Insert date	**Test performance to class – aim for a complete piece**
Insert date	Refine performance after class feedback
Insert date	**Whole piece complete**
Insert date	Deadline for props, set and design to be in place
Insert date	**'Mock' exam performance with a test audience**
Insert date	Final run in the space – make any changes from 'mock' audience feedback
Insert date	**Get-in**
Insert date	Technical rehearsal
Insert date	**Dress rehearsal – get a final test audience in to watch**
Insert date	Final examined performance

COMPONENT 1: DEVISING

Rehearsal tips

Your final piece must be rehearsed, not improvised. Keeping momentum and making rehearsals continually useful is not easy.

You may be going over the same work again and again and you could become half-hearted and find yourself going through the motions, especially if your group is working alone in the space.

Salem State University theatre students during a play rehearsal

Some suggestions to help you to make the most of the rehearsals are:

- Swap roles – seeing someone else do your role might give you a new perspective on it and then you can apply this when you take the role back yourself
- Record and watch back rehearsals – no one likes to see or hear themselves, or their work, but it is really useful once you get over any initial embarrassment
- Seek motivation in each other – work as team and be positive towards each other
- Come to the rehearsals with energy
- Step out of the performance and watch it, then offer feedback
- Get people you trust to act as a test audience – this will help you to control nerves and also they should be asked for their feedback which you can then use to improve the work
- Set objectives for the rehearsal: 'by the end of this session we want to…' and then evaluate how well you have done and re-set objectives at the end
- Do speed-runs at times to help with lines and blocking
- Don't always begin rehearsing from the start of the performance.

Health and Safety

Your performance must show that you have understood and adhered to all relevant health and safety rules. In your portfolio, if you are a design candidate, wherever relevant you draw attention to these considerations and rules.

What you will need to consider will depend on what you are using within your piece, such as equipment, and the space you are using for the performance. Your teacher should be guiding you through this part of the process, but there is plenty online that you can also research for yourself.

Some of the things you will have to consider and find the rules about will be:

Electrical

All portable appliance equipment you use must have been tested by a competent person regularly. It should have a sticker on it to prove when this was last done.

Even if you see that this sticker is current for the year, you should still always complete your own visual check before using the equipment.

Any fixed and permanently wired installations, such as the lighting rig, must also have been inspected regularly and again there should be certificates and a sticker on the equipment to show that this is the case.

Your group must ensure if you are using stage lighting that it is rigged correctly, with the lights being secured by chains or cable ties, for example.

Any floor lighting will have cables attached, which must be tidy.

With any electrical equipment, never work on it while it is 'live'. Ensure equipment is first switched off and disconnected before any work commences.

In some cases, an unqualified person, or a student below a certain age, is not permitted to directly operate or set up the equipment, and you might only be able to direct someone else to do this for you. The work would still be credited as yours, though, for the purposes of the assessment. If you are not sure about any aspect, ask a teacher.

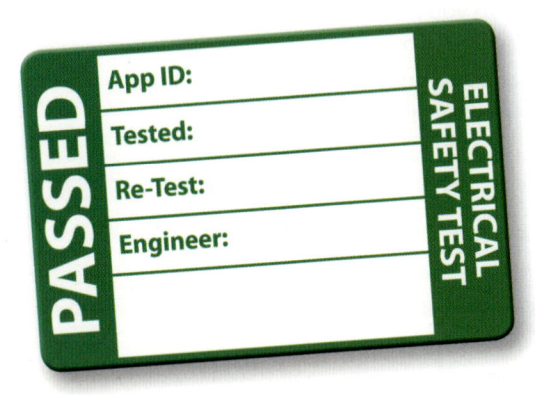

Working at height

Working at height is a high-risk activity and the risks must be effectively and consistently controlled.

The main hazards from working at height are:

- Falls
- Falling objects
- Falls from collapsing structures

All working at height activities must be risk assessed by a trained risk assessor – this is not therefore something a student can or should work on alone.

All work at height equipment must be suitable for the purpose required and inspected before each use.

While it may look great fun when you see Tallescopes or tower scaffolding in a theatre space, only trained and qualified persons can use this equipment.

Jane Eyre at the National Theatre, 2015

Special effects – smoke machines

If you wish to use a smoke machine in your performance it must be tested (as with all electrical equipment) and it must be set up in a ventilated area with the minimum possible amount of smoke used for the effect.

If the production uses oil-based smoke machines they can create a slippery residue on floors which you must be aware of.

Sound equipment

Again, as with all electrical equipment, this must have been tested and have the relevant certification and stickers to show when the last inspection was and that the equipment passed.

In terms of using speakers, ensure they are secure, whether on a bracket or floor. Their cables must be tidy to avoid any trip hazard. The volume has regulations as well which you must take note of and you could mention this within your portfolio.

Make-up and costume

Even something as apparently 'low-risk' as this area has health and safety guidance that you must take into account.

Attention should be paid to hygiene issues when using make-up; cleaning applicators properly is important and sharing sponges and other make-up applicators should be discouraged. Make sure you know of any skin allergies the cast has if you are responsible for doing their make-up. You might need to check the contents of the products you are using to be sure.

WEBLINKS:

For more guidance on each area, the following websites are useful:

- The Association of Theatre Technicians: www.abtt.org.uk
- Health and Safety Executive: www.hse.gov.uk

The performance

You have to show your work to a live audience, which might involve:

Performing to the rest of the class or another class within the school

OR

Performing to an invited external audience

The performance must be videoed – your teacher will help you to arrange this, and there are more details about what to expect on the day on page 38 of this book.

If you are a performance candidate, you will be assessed on your ability to realise artistic intentions through:

- Use of vocal and physical skills
- Creation of character
- Communication of creative intent to an audience
- Understanding of style, genre and theatrical conventions.

If you are a design candidate, you will be assessed on your ability to realise artistic intentions through:

- Use of design skills to contribute to and support the performance as a whole
- Communication of creative intent to an audience
- Understanding of practical application and production elements.

If you are a design candidate, your design must be clearly seen in the performance as a whole. You need to work closely with the group throughout the devising process. You are assessed on your design skill rather than your competency in operating or using equipment. Design and acting should complement each other for everyone to gain marks.

If no one is being marked as a design candidate in your group you can still use design elements in your piece, but ensure you put your time and energy into what you are actually getting marked on.

Your teacher is allowed to give you a certain level of support and guidance throughout the development of the performance but, as you would expect, they can't do so during the actual performance. They can also give you feedback, once, after you have completed a full first draft of your portfolio, and then you can re-draft the work.

> See pages 40-45 for more details on building your portfolio.

COMPONENT 1: DEVISING

How am I marked for the performance?

You will either have a role as a performer or in design and the final performance is worth 15 marks.

Your teacher awards you the marks; these are moderated later by the exam board using the video recording that is made of the final performance.

Here is the part of the assessment criteria which applies in the performance of the final devised piece. 'AO' is short for 'Assessment Objective' and is the overall aim you are trying to achieve:

AO2	Apply theatrical skills to realise artistic intentions in live performance	15 marks

If you are a performer, your teacher will award a number of the 15 available marks based on how well you have:

- demonstrated the ability to combine and apply vocal and physical skills
- demonstrated control over clarity, pace, **inflection**, pitch and **projection** in your vocal work
- shown physical control in your use of space, gesture, stillness and **stance**
- created a character or characters that support the communication of creative intent to the audience, and how focussed, confident, energetic and committed you are in sustaining a range of moods and emotions
- demonstrated an understanding of style, **genre** and theatrical conventions.

If you are being marked as a designer, your teacher is looking for how well you have:

- created a design for the performance that demonstrates your ability to combine and apply design skills
- used visual or audio elements to enhance mood, atmosphere and style, and created impact
- demonstrated the ability to design creatively within the time and resource constraints
- demonstrated an ability to create a design that supports the performers and the communication of intent to the audience, and the level of creativity and refinement
- demonstrated understanding of the practical application of materials and production elements in the performance.

IN THE REHEARSAL ROOM:

To gain the highest marks, you must show all of the above to a level that is accomplished, assured and comprehensive: so while you are rehearsing your work, keep checking back to these lists and ask yourself, 'am I covering all these points in the best way that I can?'

On the day

It is natural that you will be nervous. Nerves are actually a vital part of the process. Accept them. Control and use them.

Try to eat – but avoid things that are bad for your voice, like chocolate. Ensure you drink plenty of water as nerves will make you sweat and dehydrate.

If you are a designer in the piece, ensure you have completed all health and safety checks and that the equipment you are using is working as you expect.

Complete a warm-up as a group to ensure you are vocally and physically ready, and that you are focussed.

Though you will have rehearsed the piece many times, this is live theatre and things don't always run smoothly, no matter how hard everyone tries. If you do forget a line during the performance, work as team to get through the mistake. Stay focussed and in-role; more often than not, no one will even have noticed. Move on, and so will the audience.

Recording

The work must be recorded and may be sent to a moderator who will use the recording to check that they agree with your teacher's marks for the performance.

The recording must be complete and unedited.

The camera needs to be positioned to ensure an unobstructed and best possible recording is made of the performance.

Each student must introduce themselves at the start of the recording. You need to

- State your name and candidate number
- State what your role is as performer or designer.

Practise this in your final dress and technical rehearsals, you are performing from the moment that you come on stage and it is important to make a good first impression.

TOP TIP:

Ensure your costume means you can easily be identified. Wearing masks and black might work for the production, for example, but if this is how you appear throughout then it makes it unnecessarily difficult to identify who is playing which role, when you are being marked.

Audience

Make sure that the audience is aware that this is for assessment. They need to react positively to your work by being supportive and encouraging, but not so enthusiastic that they put you off.

Everybody present in the space will want you to do well and your teacher will be looking for every opportunity to give you positive marks for your work. **Good luck!**

Working as a Designer for Component 1: Devising

The devising unit of your GCSE is an exciting opportunity to work creatively as a group. For this unit you may wish to work as a designer focusing on one of the following areas:

- Costume
- Lighting
- Set
- Sound

For this unit you are allowed to have one designer per role, per group. Working as a designer gives you the opportunity to learn about other areas of theatre than acting. This is ideal for those who are interested in the backstage world of theatre. These roles also give you the space to work independently within your group.

> Turn to pages 154-171 for details on the particular skills that you require to work as a designer.

What do I need to do as a designer in this component?

To work as a designer for the devising component, your final design must be used in the devised performance, leading up to which you will need to:

- Complete a design for your chosen area: more details on this are provided in the technical sections of this book: pages 154-171. Once you've designed your costume or set you can have help to make it – don't worry. It's your design that's assessed, not your making of it.
- Complete the paperwork alongside your design, such as **cue sheets** and **ground plans** (don't worry, these are explained later too).
- Supervise or be involved with the making of your design, such as a costume, a piece of set, or the putting up of your chosen lights.

Is there any written work?

Yes, alongside your design you need to put together a portfolio explaining where your ideas for your design came from and how you put them together.

This is worth 45 marks so it's worth spending some time over it. Your work can be any one or a mixture of written, typed and presented as a video diary. There are plenty of options for making it suit your own style of working.

You will need to:

- show that you have thought about the **genre,** structure, character, form, style, and language of the devised piece
- write about your intentions for your design, and whether you were able to meet them
- show that you have thought about health and safety issues.

The portfolio

The portfolio, worth 45 marks, is a vital part of this component. It can take different formats:

Handwritten or typed evidence between 1500-2000 words

OR

Recorded verbal evidence between 8-10 minutes

OR

A combination of handwritten or typed evidence (between 750-1000 words) and recorded verbal evidence (between 4-5 minutes)

You cannot gain the highest marks if you have not written to the upper word limits, however, writing a lot will not gain you the marks alone – it must be of good quality.

Like the performance, the portfolio is marked by your teacher and may be sent to the exam board for moderation. If yours is chosen, read nothing into this – it is done at random by the exam board computer.

Contents of the portfolio

The portfolio is meant to outline the practical creation and development of ideas, along with an analysis and evaluation of the process and of your final performance piece.

You **must** address the following questions:

1. What was your initial response to the stimuli and what were your intentions for the piece?
2. What work did your group do in order to explore the stimuli and start to create ideas for performance?
3. What were some of the significant moments during the development process and when rehearsing and refining your work?
4. How did you consider genre, structure, character, form, style and language throughout the process?
5. How effective was your contribution to the final performance?
6. Were you successful in what you set out to achieve?

It must cover:

- Your contribution to the creation, development and realisation of the performance piece
- Consideration of **genre**, structure, character, form, style and language
- A clear outline of your intentions for the piece
- An understanding of any relevant health and safety issues.

You can include:

- Notes and annotated text
- Audio and/or video evidence
- Annotated drawings and sketches
- Annotated photographs
- Extended written responses
- Extra research.

COMPONENT 1: DEVISING

When should I start my portfolio?

Keep recording what happens at each stage of developing the piece of work; don't rely on your memory by starting the portfolio at the end of the process.

Type up or write down everything that happens and then edit and select once the process is complete.

In terms of the style for recording the notes during the process, you might choose to record what happens in a diary format to be edited and moved around when you are finalising the portfolio. Alternatively, you might choose to record what happens under key headings.

Here is an example of how you might record notes in a diary style:

- Mention names for who did what – especially yourself
- Keep research and other evidence in a folder
- Include Date
- The sequence of what happened is clear in its description

Thursday 6 November

Liv had brought in some research on Hitler's childhood. It was biographical, from the internet. We took the text – there was a lot (copy is in folder) – and reduced it to key moments in his life (my suggestion).

We underlined the sheet at first to pick the key moments. Then we discussed what we had chosen and we wrote out the final 10 key moments (copy is in folder). Making the choice of just 10 was difficult.

I suggested we could add or cut the number later if we needed to. Our piece is not just about Hitler, therefore we don't want to have too much on his life.

We then turned the 10 key moments into a series of still images to move it from research to something visual for performance. I have taken pictures and they are on the computer – could be used and annotated in final portfolio. I was especially vocal in offering ideas for images 3, 4 and 7. I said the use of proxemics in image 3 could really communicate how isolated Hitler felt at that moment. I thought image 6 was very effective – Henry's facial expression showed a building rage, and he had closed-off body language to communicate how he was feeling in relation to those around him.

We wanted to show more depth to Hitler and to make the audience question what they knew about him.

- Ideas are justified – including consideration of impact on audience and aims of the piece
- Take pictures as evidence and to remind you of the work you did at each stage
- There is analysis and evaluation

Evaluating your contribution to the final performance

A crucial aspect of the portfolio is evaluating the performance that you have created and been part of. You have to do this in terms of evaluating your own contribution to the process and the performance.

You also have to analyse and evaluate whether your group's aims and intentions for the piece and audience have been met.

When considering and evaluating your own impact on the final performance, look back at your notes and all the times you made suggestions:

- What were your best contributions in the process that moved the work forward in some way?
- How did you work with the stimuli and what were your reactions to them?
- What research did you do?
- How did you develop your character?
- What did you change physically in order to play the character?
- How did you develop someone else's performance?
- How could you have improved your performance in the final piece?
- What did you do outside of lessons that helped the piece come together?
- How did your contributions link to the aims of the piece?

The Red Shoes, by Kneehigh, 2010

COMPONENT 1: DEVISING

To help you analyse and evaluate whether your group's aims and intentions for the piece and audience have been met, why not consider asking your audience for their feedback?

You could interview them afterwards, or maybe make an audience feedback and evaluation sheet for them to complete. Here is a possible design for this:

Please write your name if you are happy for us to know that this feedback came from you:

_____

Could you please outline what you thought the piece was about:

_____
_____
_____

In terms of the characters in the piece, please write down one that you thought was especially convincing. Please say what was good about the role and what the student did that made it effective as a performance.

Things you might comment on could be: use of voice – pitch, tone, volume, accent, pause, pace; use of physicality – movement, posture, gesture, facial expression, eye contact, body language, use of space

_____
_____
_____

Is there a character that you felt was under-developed? If so, please tell us which one this was and things we might like to consider to improve the role/performance.

_____
_____
_____

Which moment did you especially like and why?

_____
_____
_____

Was there something that you felt didn't work? Can you think how we might have improved this?

_____
_____
_____

How do I lay out my final portfolio?

If you are producing a written portfolio, it is advisable to type the work so that once you have had feedback from your teacher you can make changes more easily.

You could scan in or draw sketches. You could use the questions on page 40 of this book as headings and then offer examples under each heading. You could choose to have a more flowing style to the portfolio which addresses the questions within the body of writing as a whole.

Remember, you don't need to include everything that happened in your final portfolio: select from your notes the most significant moments for each heading or question.

You must use appropriate subject-specific terminology in your writing or speaking.

> **If you are looking for technical terms for some of the things you have learnt or applied in your devised performance, turn to the glossary on page 172 of this book. It will remind you what some of the terms are, and explain what they mean.**

Using pictures that you took during the process, or that were taken of the final performance, could help you to communicate what you mean and save you words. Remember to take good clear pictures as you are working so that they come across clearly and well. These pictures could be annotated with key drama language in text boxes around the images.

You are also allowed to record evidence instead of writing it: you might talk to camera, explaining your process, and make a slideshow of images from your rehearsal process which you speak over and annotate on screen to illustrate your points.

A checklist for your portfolio

- [ ] Have you addressed every one of the six questions on page 40 of this book?
- [ ] Have you been selective and picked the best examples rather than trying to cover everything?
- [ ] Have you included an outline of the stimuli you used and your reactions to them?
- [ ] Have you used key drama terms as much as you can, to describe, analyse and evaluate the work?
- [ ] Have you made the majority of the portfolio about the process rather than evaluating the performance? Remember – more marks are awarded for discussing the process than the evaluation.
- [ ] Have you justified what you have written?
- [ ] Have you analysed how and why rather than just described what you did?
- [ ] Have you evaluated what was good and less good in your work?
- [ ] Have you continually outlined what you did in the process and performance?
- [ ] Have you been clear on what the aims were and whether they have been met?
- [ ] Have you remembered to discuss health and safety where relevant?
- [ ] Have you responded to teacher feedback when re-drafting? Remember, you will only be given feedback once, so check your redrafting carefully yourself.

COMPONENT 1: DEVISING

How am I marked for the portfolio?

The assessment criteria for the portfolio are broken into two parts:

AO1	Create and develop ideas to communicate meaning for theatrical performance	30 marks
AO4	Analyse and evaluate own work	15 marks

'Create and develop ideas to communicate meaning for theatrical performance' is marked by your teacher based on how well you have:

- explained the creative intentions for the piece
- explained the way you created, developed and refined ideas from the stimuli in order to communicate meaning
- written about your engagement with the process of collaboration, rehearsal and refinement
- used drama terminology.

'Analyse and evaluate own work' is marked by your teacher based on how well you have:

- analysed and evaluated your personal contribution to the creation, development and refinement process
- analysed and evaluated decisions made regarding content, **genre**, structure, character, form, style and language
- analysed and evaluated your own performance skills or design skills as shown in the final performance
- analysed and evaluated your personal contribution and the realisation of creative intentions in the performance.

ANALYSIS v. EVALUATION

You will have noticed that you're always being asked to make sure you **analyse and evaluate** your work. Ensure that you're clear on the difference between these two things:

ANALYSE means looking at how something was done. How did you go about exploring the stimuli you were given, or researching? How did you show that your character was hurt, or jealous?

EVALUATE means looking at how effective something was. Was all of your practical exploration useful or did you get more out of working with still images than hot-seating? Did your design concept for the final performance come off as you hoped or were there things you would make clearer if you could do it again?

Component 2

Performance from Text

People love stories. We enjoy watching and hearing well-told performances of comedies, tragedies, warnings, moral lessons, revenge, mistakes, crimes, betrayal, hate, love, war and struggles against injustice, presented on stage and film.

Drama performed for an audience may be in the form of a play, musical, dance, circus, mime or a mix of genres. Text is the written outline and details what the performance is or was. It can be revisited, re-interpreted and performed in every possible way.

Since early Greek theatre, playwrights have written down the two key elements of their drama ideas:

- speeches for their characters, and
- instructions on how they should move about the stage

WHY DO I NEED TO KNOW THIS?

This component asks you to show you understand how to make a performance from texts, from different time periods and different cultures, as a performer and/or a designer.

It wants you to show how characters are made, how they express opinion, conflict, affection and dislike on stage. You need to know how a plot works in a drama and how it can be brought to life in a way that will stir emotion, spread empathy, generate loathing or amusement, or create a desire to do something about a cause.

Some examples

The German playwright Bertolt Brecht (1898-1956) believed his audiences should not get emotionally attached to characters but should want to do something about an issue – change something in society that's wrong. John Godber (b.1956) used his dramas to put across a view that's often political and hoping for change, but in such a comedic way that some members of the audience think they have only seen a comedy.

Blood Brothers was originally a play, then music was added to make it a conventional piece of musical theatre, yet it's still a drama that appeals to audiences of all ages and lasts for generations. *Les Miserables*, one of the all-time successful musicals and later a film, started as a novel.

So, texts are written frameworks of the drama. Directors, designers, writers and actors can pick them up and rework them or create a fresh production. That is how drama is made.

Do I have to study lots of plays?

It's a good idea to read and see many different texts being performed, but for this component you will need to study one text, interpret it, rehearse it, polish it and perform two key extracts from it OR create a design to interpret the performed extracts.

COMPONENT 2: PERFORMANCE FROM TEXT

Component 2: key facts

This component accounts for 20% of your GCSE and is worth 48 marks.

You'll have to do one of the following:

- interpret, explore and perform two key extracts from a text your school has chosen

OR

- interpret, explore and design two key extracts from a text your school has chosen

OR

- interpret, explore and perform one key extract from a text your school has chosen and interpret, explore and design for a second extract.

> See page 65 for details of design roles in this component. As always, you can choose to specialise in costume, lighting, set or sound. Each of these is explored in detail in pages 154-171 of this book.

A visiting examiner will watch your work to assess whether you can apply theatrical skills to realise artistic intentions in live performance as a performer and/or as a designer.

Can my school choose any play?

The full text must have been professionally commissioned and/or performed and be at least 45 minutes long. It must give all students the opportunity to show exploratory range and depth, contain some sense of challenge and be appropriate in content, theme and context.

What's a key extract?

It's a scene or moment that's significant to the text as a whole. Your two extracts could be continuous dialogue, consecutive scenes or separate moments with or without a link, but it must be clear where each extract begins and ends.

Extracts can be edited to match the number of students in your group, and a group can be as small as one student performing a monologue. A monologue or duologue can also be edited but must make sense.

Groups in your school can choose different texts from each other, and you can perform different roles in your own two extracts, but they must both be from the same playtext.

How big can a group be, and how long do we have to perform for?

A group must be between 3 and 6 performance students, and one designer is allowed per design role. Timings are strict and you will lose marks if your piece does not fall into these limits:

- For one student (a monologue) you must perform for 2-3 minutes per extract
- Two performers (a duologue), must produce 3-5 minutes per extract
- 3-4 performers must produce 10-12 minutes per extract
- 5-6 performers must produce 13-15 minutes per extract

These timings ensure that every student has time to be assessed for their work by the examiner during the performance.

Case studies

This chapter will take the form of case studies. These will not necessarily match your teacher's choice of texts. Your school or college will have a free choice of which text to choose for you to explore and perform two extracts from, provided it's not from the list of set texts for component 3 and that it contrasts with the text you are studying in component 3 – in terms of its writer, period and genre.

To help you prepare, we are looking at extracts from *One Man, Two Guvnors* as an example of group performance, and some strong duologues and monologues from Shakespeare's *Macbeth*. Though these may not be your own teacher's choice of texts, you can use these case studies to learn how texts are used for group and duologue or monologue performances and what the examiner will be looking for.

How do we go about doing this component?

1. Read the full play text so that you understand the context of your extract.
2. Read through your extract as a group several times, trying different students in different roles
3. Decide who is who, read again to be certain
4. Block the moves in carefully – remember audience sightlines and especially the examiner, who will sit in the centre
5. Take advice from your teacher(s)
6. Video some rehearsals to self-improve
7. Ask for peer advice
8. Rehearse, rehearse, rehearse
9. Perform it as you rehearsed, and
10. Enjoy it!

Remember:

- If you are on stage but not speaking, you are still performing
- You are unlikely to over-rehearse.

Is there a written element to this component?

Before the performance, you must write a summary of your artistic intention: 100-200 words **per extract**. If you are a performer, these must answer the following questions:

- what role(s) are you playing?
- what is happening to your character(s) in the key extract?
- what are your character's objectives/motivations/feelings?
- how are you interpreting the character(s) in performance? (vocally, physically, and communicating your intent.)

If you are a designer, these are your questions:

- what design role are you fulfilling?
- what is your central design concept in the key extract?
- how have you interpreted this key extract through your design?
- what are you hoping to communicate to the audience?

COMPONENT 2: PERFORMANCE FROM TEXT

Case study 1: a group performance

DETAILS OF THE TEXT:
One Man, Two Guvnors by Richard Bean

Oberon Modern Plays, published 2011
ISBN: 978-84943-029-6

After first performances at the National Theatre, London in May 2011, this comedy transferred to London West End theatre, the Adelphi. A version opened in New York in April 2012 and a highly successful tour of the production went across the UK until spring 2015.

What's it about, in a nutshell?

Quoting from the website of the tour: 'Fired from his skiffle band, Francis Henshall becomes minder to Roscoe Crabbe. But Roscoe is really Rachel, posing as her own dead brother – who's been killed by her boyfriend Stanley Stubbers. Francis spots the chance of an extra meal ticket and takes a job with that Stanley Stubbers – but to prevent discovery, he must keep his two guvnors apart. Simple.'

One Man Two Guvnors at the National Theatre, 2001

Why might it be a good choice for my group?

Over a million people saw it and most loved it. Critically it's been described as 'a unique, laugh-out-loud mix of satire, songs, slapstick and glittering one-liners.'

It's based on the play *The Servant of Two Masters* by Carlo Goldoni (1707-1793) first performed about 1748. It's a classic example of the Italian **Commedia dell'Arte**, and *One Man, Two Guvnors* follows that same tradition.

COMMEDIA DELL'ARTE

Commedia dell'Arte is a popular form of street, open air theatre that began in Venice in the 1600s performed by travelling professional entertainers. It was based on improvised scenarios and jokes (called *lazzi*) involving stock characters based on universal types including rich, rather stupid masters such as shopkeepers or businessmen, devious servants and sexy serving maids, a young man of adventure such as a Captain, starry-eyed lovers, glamorous but unhappy wives, idiots, pompous know-alls, and often an old doctor.

The comedy was achieved by dance, music, witty dialogue and banter and all kinds of physical theatre effects, knock-about and trickery. There was much mime and sometimes masks, too. Its influence spread throughout Europe and continues to this day in art forms such as circus clowning, pantomime and Punch and Judy.

What do I need to learn about the play?

Set in 1963, there's a sense of that time rather than the contemporary, but it's very much not set in Venice in the 17th century.

You will read, study, analyse and perform enough of it to understand its themes, issues and performance conventions, particularly of your chosen extracts.

You must know the comedy **genre**, the structure of the play – how the confusions arise and how Francis Henshall the servant gets into and out of the scrapes he does.

Stage directions are important as they aid the director and actors. The language characters use and the style of the extracts help show you how a play moves from page to stage.

How the characters relate to each other, how they develop during the timeframe of the action and how meaning is communicated demonstrates your knowledge of the text.

How do I show that?

- Through your character and his or her use of voice and tone
- your use of space, levels, and **proxemics**
- your relationship with the audience and other performers
- how you use props and costumes
- how you communicate the author's intention in the extracts.

How are we marked for this?

You are marked individually, but for a group piece or duologue you have to work collaboratively to develop your ideas and interpretations. Theatre is collaboration which develops specific artistic intentions.

You will learn lines and moves, rehearse and polish your work leading up to the performance. Your teacher(s) will adopt a facilitating role and may direct and give advice during practical work and preparation for performance, but not for the performance itself.

When directing they are allowed to:

- interpret and structure the text as written to meet the demands of the examination (time limits)
- suggest solutions to artistic and creative problems, referring to the assessment criteria
- help make artistic and creative decisions, referring to the assessment criteria (however, they should not make direct judgements about the assessment criteria or allocate marks).

Before you perform, you must hand in, to be sent to the examiner, a brief written explanation of your intention for each performance. This should be only 100-200 words per extract and must include:

- what role(s) you are playing
- what is happening to your character(s) in the extract
- what their objectives/motivations/feelings are
- how you are interpreting this character in performance (vocally, physically, and communicating your intent).

Your performances will be recorded and the recordings will be taken by the examiner or sent on.

COMPONENT 2: PERFORMANCE FROM TEXT

What is the examiner looking for?

As a performer you will be assessed on each piece for:

1. Vocal and physical skills (up to 8 marks)

Vocal skills – are they secure, with an effective understanding of how actors make creative choices to communicate meaning? Is the comedy funny? Is the tragedy convincing? Have you got good technical control with clarity of voice, pace, the way you emphasise words/phrases, is it loud enough, is it varied throughout?

Physical skills – do you understand how actors' choices of movement, posture, gestures, facial expression, stillness, use of space, contact, spatial relationships and proxemics convey meaning to an audience? Is your physicality appropriate and varied?

2. Characterisation and communication (up to 8 marks)

Characterisation – does it show you understand the role of your character in the extracts in an accomplished, skilful and highly engaging way? Do you show focus, confidence and commitment throughout?

Communication – do you communicate with the audience in an assured way?

3. Artistic intention and style/genre/theatrical conventions (up to 8 marks)

Artistic intention – is your contribution to the group's realisation of the piece assured? Is your individual performance refined, articulate and dynamic – creating impact?

Style/genre/theatrical conventions – do you have control over and understanding of these aspects? Is your interpretation of the text in performance accomplished and comprehensive?

What would be a good extract?

Take Act 1 scene 4, (pages 43-46). This scene is the one that ends the first half of the play on a high note of action and comedy.

It's set in a cricket themed bar squeezed between 2 dining rooms, Bradman stage left, Compton stage right. Upstage centre, stairs go to the ground floor and kitchens. Francis Henshall, the servant, has two guvnors – Roscoe and Stanley Stubbers. He is in a panic to keep them separate.

Francis (James Corden) faces one of many challenges in *One Man, Two Guvnors*

FRANCIS: Roscoe has insisted on having lunch with Charlie, up here in private, instead of downstairs in the bar. Don't ask me why he wants to eat in private. I'm not paid to think. Mr Stubbers is having a lie down, which I guess you have to do a lot when you're *lying low*. I've been nil by mouth for sixteen hours. I'm only alive cos me gall bladder's worked out a way of eating me kidneys. But! The good news is it's lunch time. There's gonna be food everywhere, and all I've got to do is organise a stash, you know, leftovers, the odd whole course going missing. Hide it under here maybe. *(He looks under the table. Comes up with a mousetrap.)* A mouse trap with a chunk of CHESHIRE CHEESE! My favourite. All white and crumbly. And this bit's only slightly nibbled. *(He licks the cheese with an extended tongue. Enter STANLEY.)*

STANLEY: Henshall!
FRANCIS jumps in fright, the mouse trap goes off on his tongue. He takes the trap off his tongue.

FRANCIS: Aaaaargh!

STANLEY: How come a mouse trap went off on your tongue?

FRANCIS: It's a personal thing guv.

STANLEY: Understand! I too enjoy pain. Have you found Paddy?

FRANCIS: I was going to look for him after LUNCH.

STANLEY: I've got no time to waste on lunch. I'm going down to the pier to look for him myself.

FRANCIS: *(Aside.)* Now this suits me! Get this guvnor out the way while I serve the other one.

STANLEY: By the way, what does Paddy look like?

FRANCIS: He's a big lad, smells of horses.

STANLEY: Smells *of* horses? Or smells *like a* horse? The former is respectable, indicative of family money, the latter is just poor hygiene.

FRANCIS: At the end of the day, it's the same thing ain't it.

STANLEY: *(A mini epiphany*.)* Good point.

FRANCIS: Now take your time guv. There's two piers, enjoy the sunshine, I can't remember which pier he said now. Do you want me to order food for you, for later?

STANLEY: I'm not that hungry, order what you like. I need to eat in private, waited on by you and you alone. What's this Don Bradman room like? *(He looks into Bradman room.)* Perfect. I'll eat in here. *(Takes out envelope of money.)* I don't want to take all this cash with me. Can I trust you with it Henshall?

This speech is a 'direct address' to the audience.

He is very hungry, this informs his behaviour throughout the scene.

Character background.

He stresses how hungry he is.

Francis often breaks out of the action to talk direct to the audience.

Paddy doesn't exist: Francis has made him up.

COMPONENT 2: PERFORMANCE FROM TEXT

```
FRANCIS: Is it edible?
STANLEY: I doubt it.
FRANCIS: It's safe with me then guv.
STANLEY: I'll slip out the back.
    STANLEY slopes off down the service stairs. Enter GARETH and
    ALFIE. GARETH is thirty something and a trained headwaiter type.
    ALFIE is meant to be old, slow and doddery.
GARETH: My name's Gareth. I'm the head waiter. This is Alfie.      45
ALFIE: I'm eighty-six.
GARETH: No you're not. You're eighty-seven.
ALFIE: I thought I was eighty-six.
GARETH: No. That was last year. Be patient with Alfie please,
    he's a bit deaf, so don't turn your back, he's gonna lip read.   50
ALFIE: I ain't ever going back there! (To FRANCIS.) It was a
    bloody massacre.
GARETH: He was at Gallipoli*. He has balance problems, he
    suffers from the tremors, and he's got one of them new
    fangled pacemakers for his heart.
FRANCIS: Is that all I need to know?
GARETH: One other thing.
FRANCIS: What's that?
GARETH: It's his first day.
```

Many of Francis' jokes are for the audience's benefit.

This section is a build-up of comedy ideas. Timing is very important here.

*epiphany: a revelation

*Gallipoli: an extended First World War battle

This is the first part of the scene and it sets the tone for the whole thing. The situational comedy is set up with two rooms off, and the protagonist's aim to keep his guvnors apart from each other. The visual and verbal jokes about old Alfie are typical **Commedia dell'Arte** with a stereotype of a very old man who the audience know will be the butt of much humour.

If I'm playing Alfie?

You would have to play for longer than just this short extract, but overall make sure your vocal and physical skills demonstrate a deaf, 87-year old man with a heart condition and trembling hands who served in the First World War.

You'd have to make sure your body language, facial expressions, gestures, the way you walk and bent knees fully reflect the age. The **genre** is comedy, so your character must consistently allow others to laugh at you: this requires you to communicate well with the audience.

And if I'm playing Francis?

This man is a lovable rogue; he's always in immediate danger of being caught. He is a quick-witted liar and always has an excuse. Given that he must keep the guvnors apart, think how his agitation will show, and he will also have some frustration that the outwardly useless Alfie has been sent to help him serve lunch.

He hasn't eaten for 16 hours and is looking for ways to steal some food – that is his objective (see page 31 on Stanislavski). He shares thoughts with the audience, directly addressing them in **asides**.

Ask yourself the same questions as if you were playing Alfie. Are you communicating comic intention to the audience through physical, vocal and characterisation skills?

Other parts of the scene

Look at page 50. Later on in the lunch...

> *Alfie enters from the staircase panting and out of breath carrying a plate of charcuterie*.*
>
> ALFIE: Here's your cawld meats.
>
> *ALFIE hands over the plate to FRANCIS and then turns up his pacemaker.*
>
> FRANCIS: Look at that! Beautiful. Ham, beef, what do they call that sliced sausage over there?
>
> ALFIE: Pepperonly.
>
> *FRANCIS takes the charcuterie plate from ALFIE and eats a slice. ALFIE watches him.*
>
> FRANCIS: Beautiful.
> You sound out of breath Alfie?
>
> ALFIE: It's them 'kin stairs, they tek it out of yer. I'll turn mi pace mekker up a couple of notches.
>
> *FRANCIS takes the plate. STANLEY opens the door quickly, knocking ALFIE in the face. ALFIE makes a full turn and then rolls backwards down the stairs, unseen by STANLEY.*

Annotations:
- Think about accent.
- Diction is important for the audience to get each funny line.
- Francis has been building up to this moment.
- Physical comedy.

charcuterie: a selection of cooked cold meats in slices

This is getting more like **farce**, **slapstick**, or physical comedy.

If you're playing Alfie here you wheeze up the stairs, speak in some strange vocal twists, watch the servant eat some of the meat, are knocked in the face by a door and as you turn, you fall downstairs. In fact, a few moments before this moment, you fell down the stairs when Francis unbalanced you, so this is the second time in quick succession.

COMPONENT 2: PERFORMANCE FROM TEXT

Your body, in character, becomes the clown-like focus of audience laughter, especially as Stanley doesn't even notice what he's done and Francis is still enjoying the fact that he's actually eaten something.

Are you showing that you understand the genre and the style, that you are interpreting it and conveying meaning through your physical and vocal skills?

Now let's look at page 52, where Francis has just seized the opportunity to gulp from a tureen* of soup. A second tureen from the other room is now in his hands. He needs a hiding place.

FRANCIS: I need someone to look after this soup for me. *(He goes into the front row and hands the tureen to CHRISTINE, a plant*.)* You don't mind do you? What's your name?

CHRISTINE: Christine Patterson.

FRANCIS: Christine Patterson. Thanks for giving us all the info! Want to give out your National Insurance number as well? Will you look after this soup? Hide it under your seat. Thank you Christine Patterson. Don't let any of these bastards touch it. *(FRANCIS is back on stage. ALFIE arrives with the chicken balls.)* What you got there Alfie?

ALFIE: Chicken balls.

FRANCIS: How many have we got here?

ALFIE: Twelve.

FRANCIS: Right, give me three plates. *(ALFIE gives him three plates. FRANCIS dishes up four chicken balls to each plate, then eats one chicken ball with each reasoning, leaving only one on each of the plates.)* Three diners, so that's four each and none for me, or three each and three for me.

FRANCIS eats one chicken ball from each of the three plates.

ALFIE: Oi! Oi! He's eating the ...'kin chicken balls!

FRANCIS: Or two each and six for me.

FRANCIS eats another from each plate.

> This is more difficult when your audience knows everyone in the group. Think about who to invite to your performance to get the best reaction.

> Timing is important here to get the best out of the comedy.

tureen: a large soup serving bowl

plant: in theatre, a member of the cast hidden in the audience

He has nine, leaving one each for the diners. The point of this section is that it requires accurate use of real props and food OR some quality miming – either is valid.

A theatrical device is employed to have a **plant** in the audience: a member of the cast pretending to be just a member of the public. In this case, she soon gets up on stage and becomes involved in the action. It's often used in circus and comedy genres.

The climax of Act 1

By page 58, the pace has quickened and the comings and goings of characters have got faster as the need to keep Roscoe and Stubbers apart gets more difficult. Francis becomes ever more manic.

STANLEY: Henshall?

(*To Alfie.*) Where's he gone?

ALFIE: Please don't hurt me.

STANLEY, bemused, walks back into the Compton, closing the door.
FRANCIS comes out of the Bradman with the trolley.

FRANCIS: What you got there Alfie?

ALFIE: Roast potatoes.

FRANCIS: Alright! I'm coming through!

FRANCIS pushes the trolley towards Compton picking up ALFIE on to the trolley as he goes. STANLEY opens the door and they sweep past him into the room. Enter GARETH with the crêpe suzette* ingredients and equipment. Enter FRANCIS with ALFIE on his back, piggy-back style. FRANCIS unceremoniously dumps ALFIE and he falls down the stairs.

GARETH: Crêpe Suzette. When you were training in Ashby de la Zouch, did they teach you how to do a proper crêpe?

FRANCIS: Yeah. Crêpe, liqueur, matches, what could possibly go wrong? (*GARETH exits downstage.*) Christine. Now! Take this soup off the stage. (*CHRISTINE appears from behind the WG Grace* cut-out and comes down to the table.*) Do you know how to do crêpe suzette? Do you serve it and set fire to it or set fire to it and serve it, as it were? You haven't got a clue have you? Let's get you and the stash back down there.

FRANCIS steps back so that CHRISTINE can lean over and pick up the tureen. STANLEY opens the door from the Compton.

STANLEY: (*Off.*) Henshall!

FRANCIS coaches CHRISTINE to hide under the table.

FRANCIS: Hide! Get down!

STANLEY: Problem! This wine cannot be Grand Cru. Taste that. (*STANLEY gives FRANCIS a glass which FRANCIS downs in one.*) What do you reckons? Is it Papes?

FRANCIS: No. Actually I think it's quite good.

STANLEY: Ah! Crêpe Suzette. Go on then. I love to watch Grand Marnier* burning.
Go on. You need more than that man! (*FRANCIS drops the bottle 'spilling' liquid into the tray.*) Whoopsy daisy. (*FRANCIS lights the liqueur.*) Look at that, beautiful!
(*Flames shoot up everywhere.*)

> This is the outcome of the build up of the scene, which has been painful for Alfie. The audience must pity him as well as finding him funny.

> More physical comedy. This must be carefully rehearsed.

COMPONENT 2: PERFORMANCE FROM TEXT

> FRANCIS/STANLEY: Fire! Fire!
>   (*Christine backs out from under the table. FRANCIS chucks a jug of water over her. STANLEY gets a fire extinguisher and drenches Christine from head to toe with foam. She stands there covered in foam like an iced cake.*)
> FRANCIS: Alright. Ladies and Gentlemen! Don't worry. Nobody is injured.
>   (*Direct address.*) What I suggest we do is take a fifteen minute interval here. You can have a drink. We're going to fill out Health and Safety forms. But I did it, didn't I? I served two guvnors, and they're still none the wiser, and most important of all, I get to eat! See you in fifteen minutes. Have a good interval!
>
> *Interval.*

(Annotation: More physical comedy, particularly hilarious for the audience who do not realise she is a plant from the cast.)

(Annotation: Francis breaks the fourth wall to talk to the audience again.)

* Crêpe suzette: a sweet pancake dessert
* WG Grace: a famous cricketer, keeping the cricketing theme going
* Grand Marnier: a type of brandy

This part of the scene presents a design challenge – the fire could be projected, or mimed with everybody's response in slow motion. The water and foam could be applied before the match is struck, which might be funnier anyway – an over-reaction making Christine's drenching really comical.

The same questions must always be asked by you and your group. Are you showing that you understand the genre and the style, that you are interpreting it and conveying meaning through your physical and vocal skills?

The scene requires continuing comedic acting skills including voice and physicality, maintaining characterisation already established, the pace to be quickened, a sense of madness to take over and real communication with the audience – for instance, this is the third time Alfie falls down the stairs through no fault of his own.

One Man, Two Guvnors has a cast of about 17, but some are very minor and Francis is a dominant role. You could have smaller groups to give more people the chance to play him, or choose another play with more main parts.

Case study 2: a duologue or monologue

> **DETAILS OF THE TEXT:**
>
> ## *Macbeth* by William Shakespeare
>
> CGP Books (2012) 1977
> ISBN: 978-1-84146-120-5
>
> This edition has explanations of character development, meanings and helpful questions to ask as you rehearse.
>
> *Macbeth* is often called the 'Scottish play' because superstition has it that it's cursed, and unlucky to name it in a theatre. It's a classic tale of murder, betrayal, ambition, power, revenge and justice. It's strong, dark and powerful with interesting characters and supernatural elements.

What's it about, in a nutshell?

In medieval Scotland when Macbeth, a general in King Duncan's army, and his fellow soldier, Banquo, are returning from a successful battle, they meet three witches on a barren heath, who prophesy that Macbeth will be king.

Duncan promotes Macbeth and says he will stay the night at Macbeth's castle. Lady Macbeth comes up with a plot to murder Duncan in the night so that Macbeth can be king immediately, but fears Macbeth lacks courage to do it. She persuades him to commit the murder and frame two guards for the crime. He does indeed become king.

Macbeth soon has his friend Banquo murdered, because having heard the witches' prophesy, he knows too much. However, he then sees Banquo's ghost and starts to become unbalanced. Another nobleman called Macduff runs away to England to build an army against the new king, and while he is away, Macbeth has his wife and children killed. He seeks fresh revelation from the witches, who give him a prophesy which makes him feel safer. His wife begins sleepwalking, haunted by their crimes.

Eventually the 'safe' prophecy proves not to be as Macbeth thought and he is punished with death at the hands of Macduff.

Ian McKellen and Judi Dench in *Macbeth* at The Other Place, RSC, Stratford-upon-Avon, 1976

COMPONENT 2: PERFORMANCE FROM TEXT

Why might it be a good choice for me?
It has passages of duologue, and **soliloquys** that are challenging, absorbing and offer opportunities for a character really to develop.

It's written in **blank verse**, a poetic, rhythmic form of speech which adds to the drama.

Its timeless themes are the stuff of good theatre.

The characters – Macbeth and his scheming wife, the murdered friend and ghost Banquo and the three witches all offer excellent dramatic possibilities as characters under stress.

There is also a comedy section where the drunken gate keeper or Porter gives a mini monologue and short duologue as relief from the violence and death.

Written between 1603 and 1607 and based on a real person, it's anything but a dry and dusty piece of old drama. It's an outstanding tragedy, one of Shakespeare's most popular, and a template for many dramas since.

For a student serious about performing a stunning piece of drama in duologue or monologue, it's a strong choice. It's also a good choice for group extracts.

What do I need to learn about the play?

You must read, study, analyse and perform enough of the play to understand its themes, issues and performance conventions, particularly those of your chosen extracts.

You must understand the **tragedy** genre: the structure of the play – how the prophecies from the supernatural witches come to pass and how murder and treachery do not go unpunished.

Stage directions aid the director and actors, but there are only a few in Shakespeare's plays: the language characters use help show you how a play moves from page to stage.

How the characters relate to each other, how they develop during the timeframe of the action and how meaning is communicated demonstrates your knowledge of the text.

How do I show that?
- Your character and his or her use of voice and tone
- your use of space, levels, **proxemics**
- your relationship with the audience and the other performer (in a duologue)
- how you use props and costumes
- how you communicate the author's intention in the extracts.

How am I marked for this?
Your teacher(s) will adopt a facilitating and supervisory role in your pieces and they can direct you during your development phase.

You will learn lines and moves, rehearse and polish your work and then perform it live.

CASE STUDY 2: A DUOLOGUE OR MONOLOGUE

Before you perform, you must hand in a brief written explanation of your intention for each performance. This should be only 100-200 words per extract and must include:

- what role(s) you are playing
- what is happening to your character(s) in the extract
- what their objectives/motivations/feelings are
- how you are interpreting this character in performance (vocally, physically, and communicating your intent).

Your performances will be recorded and the recordings will be taken by the examiner or sent on.

What is the examiner looking for?

As a performer you will be assessed on each piece for:

1. Vocal and physical skills (up to 8 marks)

Vocal skills – are they secure, with an effective understanding of how actors make creative choices to communicate meaning? Is the comedy funny? Is the tragedy convincing? Have you got good technical control with clarity of voice, pace, the way you emphasise words/phrases, is it loud enough, is it varied throughout?

Physical skills – do you understand how actors' choices of movement, posture, gestures, facial expression, stillness, use of space, contact, spatial relationships and **proxemics** convey meaning to an audience? Is your physicality appropriate and varied?

2. Characterisation and communication (up to 8 marks)

Characterisation – does it show you understand the role of your character in the extracts in an accomplished, skilful and highly engaging way? Do you show focus, confidence and commitment throughout?

Communication – do you communicate with the audience in an assured way?

3. Artistic intention and style/genre/theatrical conventions (up to 8 marks)

Artistic intention – is your contribution to the realisation of the piece assured? Is your performance refined, articulate and dynamic – creating impact?

Style/genre/theatrical conventions – do you have control over and understanding of these aspects? Is your interpretation of the text in performance accomplished and comprehensive?

What would be a good duologue extract?

Act 2 scene 2: the scene immediately after Macbeth has murdered King Duncan.

Macbeth's castle; enter Lady Macbeth

LADY MACBETH: That which hath made them drunk, hath made me bold;
What hath quench'd them, hath given me fire.

An owl shrieks.

> She has been drinking alcohol before this scene.

> This sound effect heightens the tension in the scene.

COMPONENT 2: PERFORMANCE FROM TEXT

> Hark, peace!
> It was the owl that shriek'd, the fatal bellman*
> Which gives the stern'st good-night. He is about it. 5
> The doors are open, and the surfeited grooms
> Do mock their charge with snores. I have drugg'd their possets*
> That death and nature do contend about them,
> Whether they live, or die.

MACBETH: *(Off.)* Who's there? What ho? *[Macbeth is nervous.]*

LADY MACBETH: Alack, I am afraid they have awak'd,
And 'tis not done; th'attempt and not the deed
Confounds us. Hark! I laid their daggers ready,
He could not miss 'em. Had he not resembled
My father as he slept, I had done't. 15

Enter Macbeth with two bloody daggers.
My husband? *[What does this tell us about Lady Macbeth's character?]*

MACBETH: I have done the deed. Didst thou not hear a noise?

LADY MACBETH: I heard the owl scream and the crickets cry.
Did you not speak?

MACBETH: When? 20

LADY MACBETH: Now.

MACBETH: As I descended? *[This short, snappy exchange heightens the tension.]*

LADY MACBETH: Ay.

MACBETH: Hark!
Who lies i' th' second chamber? 25

LADY MACBETH: Donalbain.

MACBETH: *(Looking at his hands)* This is a sorry sight. *[He has blood on his hands.]*

LADY MACBETH: A foolish thought, to say a sorry sight.

MACBETH: There's one did laugh in's sleep, and one cried 'Murder!'
That they did wake each other – I stood and heard them, 30
But they did say their prayers, and addressed them
Again to sleep.

LADY MACBETH: There are two lodged together.

MACBETH: One cried 'God bless us!' And 'Amen' the other,
As they had seen me with these hangman's hands.
List'ning their fear, I could not say 'Amen' *[Macbeth is afraid that he will be punished by God. This also heightens his tension.]*
When they did say 'God bless us.'

LADY MACBETH: Consider it not so deeply.

bellman: a man who sounds each of the hours with a bell through the night

possets: drinks

CASE STUDY 2: A DUOLOGUE OR MONOLOGUE

GCSE DRAMA STUDY GUIDE

The image of bloody hands, or 'these hangman's hands' is powerful and occurs several times in the play.

Lady Macbeth can be played a number of ways in this scene. When she says 'consider it not deeply,' she is dismissing his fears, but does she feel so sure herself?

The relationship between Macbeth and his wife is powerfully portrayed as she takes charge, yet they whisper in short phrases in the night, in fear of being discovered or overheard.

She must use **direct address** before switching to duologue with her husband. She has been drinking but still is in control. At this stage she maintains a clear-head and an ability to think through how they might get away with murder by blaming others. She later says that 'the sleeping and the dead are but as pictures' – reassuring her husband that there's no need to fear them.

Other duologues from the play

- Act 1 scene 7, Macbeth and Lady Macbeth, planning to kill Duncan
- Act 2 scene 4, Ross and an Old Man discuss what's happened since Duncan's murder
- Act 3 scene 2, Lady Macbeth and Macbeth feel insecure, he feels guilty
- Act 4 scene 3, Macduff persuades Duncan's son, Malcolm, to return from England; he tests Macduff's loyalty.

What would be a good monologue?

A monologue is a fantastic opportunity to showcase your acting skills. You must reveal the artistic intentions of the extract and communicate with your audience.

Many of Shakespeare's monologues are in fact **soliloquies**, thought aloud or addressed to the audience. Think about how the layout of the Globe and other Elizabethan theatres (see page 11 of this book) might have helped this.

Here is Act 1, scene 5: Lady Macbeth has received news from Macbeth of his success in battle, his promotion, and his encounter with the witches.

> *Macbeth's castle, enter Lady Macbeth with a letter.*
>
> LADY MACBETH: 'They met me in the day of success, and I have learned by the perfectest report, they have more in them than mortal knowledge. When I burned in desire to question them further, they made themselves air, into which they vanished. Whiles I stood rapt in the wonder of it, came missives from the king, who all-hailed me Thane of Cawdor, by which title before these weird sisters saluted me, and referred me to the coming on of time with 'Hail, king that shalt be!' This have I thought good to deliver thee, my dearest partner of greatness, that thou mightst not lose the dues of rejoicing by being ignorant of what greatness is promised thee. Lay it to thy heart, and farewell.'

She is reading aloud the letter in her hand.

COMPONENT 2: PERFORMANCE FROM TEXT

> Glamis thou art, and Cawdor, and shalt be
> What thou art promised; yet do I fear thy nature,
> It is too full o'th'milk of human kindness
> To catch the nearest way. Thou wouldst be great,
> Art not without ambition, but without
> The illness should attend it. What thou wouldst highly,
> That wouldst thou holily; wouldst not play false,
> And yet wouldst wrongly win. Thou'dst have, great Glamis,
> That which cries, 'Thus thou must do,' if thou have it;
> And that which rather thou dost fear to do,
> Than wishest should be undone. Hie thee hither,
> That I may pour my spirits in thine ear   25
> And chastise with the valour of my tongue
> All that impedes thee from the golden round,
> Which fate and metaphysical* aid doth seem
> To have thee crowned withal.

- *For the rest of the speech she is speaking to Macbeth directly in her imagination.* (arrow to line 2)
- *Lady Macbeth's ambition is more like an 'illness'.* (arrow to "illness")
- *The king's crown.* (arrow to "golden round")
- *The witches.* (arrow to "metaphysical")

A messenger telling her Duncan is arriving with Macbeth tonight can be edited out. She continues speaking alone in her monologue:

> The raven himself is hoarse,   30
> That croaks the fatal entrance of Duncan
> Under my battlements. Come, you spirits
> That tend on mortal thoughts, unsex me here
> And fill me from the crown to the toe topfull
> Of direst cruelty; make thick my blood,
> Stop up th'access and passage to remorse
> That no compunctious visitings of nature
> Shake my fell purpose nor keep peace between
> Th'effect and it. Come to my woman's breasts
> And take my milk for gall*, you murd'ring ministers,
> Wherever in your sightless substances
> You wait on nature's mischief. Come, thick night,
> And pall thee in the dunnest* smoke of hell,
> That my keen knife see not the wound it makes,
> Nor heaven peep through the blanket of the dark,   45
> To cry, 'Hold, hold.'

- *She is no longer talking to Macbeth, but summoning evil spirits and asking for their help in making her cruel, so that she can persuade Macbeth to kill King Duncan.* (arrow to "Come, you spirits")

*metaphysical: supernatural

*gall: acid

*dunnest: darkest

The challenge here is to bring to life the reading of a letter followed by what is almost a prayer to dark forces to 'unsex' her: to take away the virtues of mercy and care usually associated with women, so that she can be filled with 'direst cruelty.'

Other monologues from the play

- Act 1 scene 7, Macbeth, with Lady Macbeth edited out, agreeing to the murder plan despite initially talking himself out of it.
- Act 2 scene 1, Macbeth has vision of a dagger, a short monologue.
- Act 5 scene 3 would need editing, monologues from Macbeth as his enemies close in on him.
- Act 5 scene 5 with Act 5 scene 8, edited: leading to Macbeth's death.

A monologue and duologue checklist

- [ ] Make sure your vocal skills are appropriate for the role in terms of age, status, what has just happened, setting, and time of day. Have you got variety and pace, are you loud enough?
- [ ] Then check your physical skills in the character – how old, what status, what has he or she just done, what will they do next, what effect should they have on the audience?
- [ ] Your characterisation – do you clearly show the role in terms of status, importance to the plot, do you show focus and commitment? How does the audience relate to your character through the way you are communicating him or her?
- [ ] Do you understand the artistic intention of the play as a whole and your extract in particular? Have you understood the genre, the style of performance, any theatrical conventions, do you use direct address effectively and is your interpretation accomplished and comprehensive?
- [ ] Always ask for the views of your teacher and your peers, and self-criticise through recordings of your piece before the exam. You must polish it until you live it, and perform with appropriate energy, life, pace, movement and belief.

COMPONENT 2: PERFORMANCE FROM TEXT

Working as a Designer for Component 2: Performance from Text

This unit gives you the opportunity to work with two extracts from a pre-written play and to explore them through the rehearsal period for performance – just like theatre companies do. You may wish to work as a designer focusing on one of the following areas:

- Costume
- Lighting
- Set
- Sound

For this unit you are allowed to have one designer per role per group. It is also possible to be a designer for one of your two extracts, and a performer for the other.

Working as a designer for this unit will mean that you must work collaboratively with the rest of your group of performers to create a design which suits the play that you are performing. You will need to spend time in the rehearsal room to make sure that your designs suit the way that the extracts are being performed.

> **Turn to pages 154-171 for details on the particular skills that you require to work as a designer.**

To work as a designer for the Performance from Text unit you will need to:

- Complete a design for your chosen area – more details on this are provided in the technical sections of this book, from page 154. Once you've designed your costume or set you can have help to make it – don't worry. It's your design that's assessed, not your making of it.
- Complete the paperwork alongside your design such as **cue sheets** and **ground plans** (don't worry these are explained later too).
- Supervise or be involved with the making of your design such as a costume, a piece of set or the putting up of your chosen lights.

If you are designing for one extract and performing in the second one then you will be asked to produce one costume instead of two, or the examiner will ask to see two lighting states rather than four.

How will I be assessed?

This unit is assessed by a visiting examiner who will come to your school or college to watch your performance.

Your final design must be used in the devised performance, and designers are assessed on their ability to do the following things:

- Show changes of mood and atmosphere through their designs
- Create designs that suit the style of the play studied
- Use materials practically and creatively
- Work effectively within a budget and time constraints.

Component 3

Theatre Makers in Practice

This component is the 1 hour 30 minute written examination part of the course. For the exam you will have explored practically one complete performance text, chosen from options (see page 67) by your teacher. During the exploration you will have looked into how the play text may be brought to life for an audience from the point of view of director, performer and designer. Each play is covered in the following pages of this book.

Section B: Live Theatre Evaluation is exactly as the title suggests – where you evaluate a live theatre performance you have seen. Through practice, you will have developed skills to analyse the meaning created in the performance you saw and how ideas were communicated to an audience.

Exam preparation tips

- Re-read your section A text, maybe watching a recorded version of it if one is available. Go back to notes you made at the time to remind yourself of the things you have done practically to explore the text.
- Having read the questions and answer tips in this book, try with other extracts of your choice from the play and work through them in a similar way – as a performer, director and designer. Consider each character's vocal and physical skills, and design a stage ground plan.
- Keep completing practice questions under timed conditions right up until the exam, to improve your technique and to develop your ability to respond under pressure.
- Section B – The Live Theatre Evaluation – has two questions, worth a total of 15 marks: much less than section A's unseen extract. Consider this when revising. You should spend more time preparing for section A and its 45 marks.
- You can take notes in with you for section B (see page 67 for restrictions) but these take time to re-work into a form that is really useful, so allow yourself plenty of time in the weeks before the exam to do this. Typing the notes will allow you to make last-minute changes, should you need to. You'll also be able to read them more easily in the exam.
- Clear and useful sketches or drawings in the notes, for example of the set, could be quickly copied into the exam paper if required or relevant to a question.
- Sorting the notes is not enough preparation for the exam – you can, and should 'revise' as well.

On the day

Ensure you have an idea of how much time to spend on each section, and each question within the sections, and stick to these timings in the exam.

Answer questions on ONE SET TEXT ONLY.

COMPONENT 3: THEATRE MAKERS IN PRACTICE

Component 3: key facts

This component accounts for 40% of the qualification and is worth 60 marks.

Section A: Bringing Texts to Life consists of one question broken into five parts based on an unseen extract from the text you have practically explored. Performance texts are not allowed in the examination; unseen extracts will be provided in a source booklet. The notes that you take in are only allowed to relate to Section B: Live Theatre Evaluation.

Section A

Section A is worth 45 marks, and you are recommended to spend 1 hour on this part of the exam. You will be studying only one set text, so turn to the page for your text to find sample questions and tips on writing top-band answers:

List A (pre-1954)

Performance Text	Genre	Prescribed edition*	Page
An Inspector Calls J.B Priestley	Social thriller/mystery	Heinemann ISBN 9780435232825	68
The Crucible Arthur Miller	Historical drama	Methuen (student edition) ISBM 9781408108390	77
Government Inspector Nikolai Gogol (adapted by David Harrower)	Black comedy	Faber & Faber ISBN 9780571280490	88
Twelfth Night William Shakespeare	Romantic comedy	New Longman Shakespeare ISBN 9780582365780	98

List B (post-2000)

Performance Text	Genre	Prescribed edition*	Page
DNA Dennis Kelly	Black comedy	Oberon Plays (school edition) ISBN 9781840029529	108
1984 George Orwell, Robert Icke and Duncan Macmillan	Political satire	Oberon Plays ISBN 9781783190614	117
Blue Stockings Jessica Swale	Historical drama	Nick Hern Books ISBN 9781848423299	127
Dr Korczak's Example David Grieg	Historical drama	Capercaillie Books ISBN 9780954520618	137

* The prescribed editions are the ones that will be used to reproduce the extracts for the exam.

Section B

Section B: Live Theatre Evaluation consists of two questions and is worth 15 marks. You are allowed to take in notes for this section but they must be no more than 500 words in length. You can have drawings or sketches, such as of the set, within the notes.

> **Note: Whichever text you have studied from list A or B must be in contrast with the text used for performance in Component 2. For example, if you have studied DNA by Dennis Kelly for Section A of the exam, your performance text for Component 2 must be pre-1954, and be by a different playwright and of a different genre. Don't worry – your teacher will advise you in this area.**

An Inspector Calls
by JB Priestley

The context of the play

Written in 1945, the play reflects upon the Edwardian era (1901–1914). Priestley uses the play as a method to explore his views on socialism, drawing parallels to the period he was living in. He was against the power of capitalists (traders, industrialists and businessmen) who exploited their workers.

In Edwardian England things were very difficult for the working class. Wages were poor and there was much poverty. Redundancy was common and there was no social security system – only the workhouse and charity organisations were available as support. The Edwardian era was ended by two world-shattering events: the sinking of the Titanic (a ship that was a symbol of the wealth and luxury of the time), and the outbreak of the First World War.

Priestley believed that we are all in a community and have a responsibility to look after others. His aim was to educate the audience through the characters' realisation of their roles in Eva Smith's death.

A plot summary

Spring 1912. Husband and wife, Arthur and Sybil Birling, together with their son Eric, are holding a family dinner party to celebrate their daughter Sheila's engagement to Gerald Croft.

The celebrations are interrupted by the arrival of Inspector Goole who informs the family that he is investigating the death of a girl (Eva Smith) who died two hours ago in the infirmary after committing suicide by drinking disinfectant.

One by one the assembled characters are interrogated by the mysterious Inspector and in turn each is revealed as having a part to play in Eva's death. Before leaving the party to report back, the Inspector makes a final speech with a clear moral point telling the Birlings they should not be so self-contained and to look after people who are less fortunate than themselves.

After his exit, the Birlings begin to doubt that the stranger was really from the police. Just as they are about to convince themselves that it was some horrible hoax, there is a phone call from the police informing Mr Birling that a girl has just died, while on her way to the infirmary, after swallowing disinfectant. An inspector is due to come and question them. The play ends.

DISCUSSION POINTS
Each character's guilt is easy to follow, as is their reaction to the revelation, and the play leaves its audience with much to discuss. The cliff-hanger ending leaves room for debate on meaning and who the Inspector really was.

Sheila and the Inspector in the 1954 film of *An Inspector Calls*

The characters

INSPECTOR GOOLE is a mysterious figure. He works very methodically, confronting each 'suspect' at the dinner party with a piece of information and then making them talk. His final speech is like a sermon outlining social responsibility and how the family have failed in theirs.

ARTHUR BIRLING is the owner of Birling and Company, a factory business. A social climber, he is a man of some standing in the town and he values his reputation. Underneath his confidence, he is anxious. He is unable to admit his responsibility for his part in Eva's death.

SYBIL BIRLING is a snob, and 'socially superior' to her husband. Like her husband, she is a woman of some public influence, sitting on the boards of charity organisations. She tries – unsuccessfully – to intimidate the Inspector and force him to leave. She also lies to him. She too refuses to believe that she did anything wrong and doesn't accept responsibility for her part in Eva's death.

SHEILA BIRLING, Arthur's daughter, seems very immature in the opening to the play. When Gerald eventually reveals his affair with Eva, she calls off their engagement, ruining her father's hopes of a merger between Croft's family business and his own. Following the realisation of her own part in Eva Smith's death, she matures. She feels guilt and regret and she has a new perspective on her family and judges those who remain unchanged by all that they have heard that evening.

ERIC BIRLING has a drinking problem. He works at Birling and Company. When he hears how his father sacked Eva Smith, he supports the worker's cause, like Sheila. When the truth about his relationship with Eva/Daisy is revealed, he accepts blame for his part in her death and like his sister he is 'ashamed' at his parents' and Gerald's refusal to accept responsibility.

GERALD CROFT works for his father's company, Crofts Limited. He is an aristocrat – the son of Lord and Lady Croft; they are not over-impressed by Gerald's engagement to Sheila (they declined the invitation to the celebratory dinner). When the truth about his affair with Eva/Daisy is revealed, it appears that he did have some genuine feeling for her. Despite this, he seeks to protect his own interest and deny responsibility.

Sample questions

As well as the question paper, you will get a source booklet with the extracts from each of the set texts on offer. You will only have studied one text, so find the extract you need in the source booklet and don't worry about the rest. The extract will be roughly 3 pages long in the source booklet and will link to roughly 4 pages from the copy of the text you are recommended to use in class.

In the question paper, the first line will say:

'You are involved in staging a production of this play. Please read the extract on page X of the source booklet.'

Look over the extract, which should be familiar to you from your study in class and your revision. Then begin to respond to the questions. It is recommended that you spend an hour on this section of the exam.

Remember: you are responding as a performer, director or designer. This is not English literature – it's Drama.

The sample questions on the next few pages relate to the following extract from pages 42-44 of the prescribed Heinemann edition of *An Inspector Calls*. You will need to apply the suggestions made for the sample questions to the extract and questions you are given. If your preparation and understanding is good enough, it makes no difference whether you have practised the exact questions or not, you will be able to adapt.

```
        We hear the front door slam again.
BIRLING: That was the door again.
MRS BIRLING: Gerald must have come back.
INSPECTOR: Unless your son has just gone out.
BIRLING: I'll see.
        He goes out quickly. INSPECTOR turns to MRS BIRLING
INSPECTOR: Mrs Birling, you're a member - a prominent member -     5
    of the Brumley Women's Charity Organization, aren't you?
        MRS BIRLING does not reply.
SHEILA: Go on, mother. You might as well admit it. (to INSPECTOR.)
    Yes, she is.
    Why?
INSPECTOR: (calmly) It's an organization to which women in distress 10
    can appeal for help in various forms. Isn't that so?
MRS BIRLING: (with dignity) Yes. We've done a great deal of useful
    work in helping deserving cases.
INSPECTOR: There was a meeting of the interviewing committee
    two weeks ago?                                                 15
MRS BIRLING: I dare say there was.
INSPECTOR: You know very well there was, Mrs Birling. You were
    in the chair.
MRS BIRLING: And if I was, what business is it of yours?
INSPECTOR: (Severely) Do you want me to tell you - in plain words? 20
```

Enter BIRLING, looking rather agitated.

BIRLING: That must have been Eric.

MRS BIRLING: *(alarmed)* Have you been up to his room?

BIRLING: Yes. And I called out on both landings. It must have been Eric we heard go out then.

MRS BIRLING: Silly boy! Where can he have gone to?

BIRLING: I can't imagine. But he was in one of his excitable queer moods, and even though we don't need him here –

INSPECTOR: *(cutting in, sharply)* We do need him here. And if he's not back soon, I shall have to go and find him.

BIRLING and MRS BIRLING exchange bewildered and rather frightened glances.

SHEILA: He's probably just gone to cool off. He'll be back soon.

INSPECTOR: *(severely)* I hope so.

MRS BIRLING: And why should you hope so?

INSPECTOR: I'll explain why when you've answered my questions, Mrs Birling.

BIRLING: Is there any reason why my wife should answer questions from you, Inspector?

INSPECTOR: Yes, a very good reason. You'll remember that Mr Croft told us – quite truthfully, I believe – that he hadn't spoken to or seen Eva Smith since last September. But Mrs Birling spoke to and saw her only two weeks ago.

SHEILA: *(astonished)* Mother!

BIRLING: Is this true?

MRS BIRLING: *(after a pause)* Yes, quite true.

INSPECTOR: She appealed to your organization for help?

MRS BIRLING: Yes.

INSPECTOR: Not as Eva Smith?

MRS BIRLING: No, nor as Daisy Renton.

INSPECTOR: As what then?

MRS BIRLING: First, she called herself Mrs Birling––

BIRLING: *(astounded)* Mrs Birling!

MRS BIRLING: Yes, I think it was simply a piece of gross impertinence – quite deliberate – and naturally that was one of the things that prejudiced me against her case.

BIRLING: And I should think so! Damned impudence!

INSPECTOR: You admit being prejudiced against her case?

MRS BIRLING: Yes.

SHEILA: Mother, she's just died a horrible death – don't forget.

MRS BIRLING: I'm very sorry. But I think she had only herself to blame.

INSPECTOR: Was it owing to your influence, as the most prominent member of the committee, that help was refused the girl?

MRS BIRLING: Possibly.

INSPECTOR: Was it or was it not your influence?

MRS BIRLING: *(stung)* Yes, it was. I didn't like her manner. She'd impertinently made use of our name, though she pretended afterwards it just happened to be the first she though of. She had to admit, after I began questioning her, that she had no claim to the name, that she wasn't married, and that the story she told at first – about a husband who'd deserted her was quite false. It didn't take me long to get the truth – or some of the truth – out of her.

INSPECTOR: Why did she want help?

MRS BIRLING: You know very well why she wanted help.

INSPECTOR: No, I don't. I know why she needed help. But as I wasn't there, I don't know what she asked from your committee.

MRS BIRLING: I don't think we need discuss it.

INSPECTOR: You have no hope of not discussing it, Mrs Birling.

MRS BIRLING: If you think you can bring any pressure to bear upon me, Inspector, you're quite mistaken. Unlike the other three, I did nothing I'm ashamed of or that won't bear investigation. The girl asked for assistance. We were asked to look carefully into the claims made upon us. I wasn't satisfied with the girl's claim – she seemed to me not a good case and so I used my influence to have it refused. And in spite of what's happened to the girl since, I consider I did my duty. So if I prefer not to discuss it any further, you have no power to make me change my mind.

INSPECTOR: Yes I have.

MRS BIRLING: No you haven't. Simply because I've done nothing wrong – and you know it.

INSPECTOR: *(very deliberately)* I think you did something terribly wrong – and that you're going to spend the rest of your life regretting it. I wish you'd been with me tonight in the infirmary. You'd have seen –

The first question

The first question requires you to imagine you are a performer in the play. A possible question might be:

2(a) There are specific choices in this extract for performers.

(i) You are going to play Sheila. Explain two ways you would use vocal skills to play this character in this extract. (4 marks)

COMPONENT 3: THEATRE MAKERS IN PRACTICE

For your response you will get one mark (✓) for each way identified and an additional mark (✓) for each linked explanation. For example, you might refer to:

- Pitch and tone of delivery
- Pace and volume of delivery
- Use of pause

Here are some ideas, but you wouldn't need them all - it's only a 4 mark question.
In discussing the use of voice you must demonstrate your understanding of the character as well. For example:

    (line 41) SHEILA: (astonished) Mother!

In saying this line as a performer playing Sheila you might use a louder volume ✓ to indicate your shock at finding out your mother has lied about knowing Eva Smith, and may have more secrets in regard to the woman and her death ✓.

An alternative example from the extract you might use is:

    (line 30) SHEILA: He's probably just gone to cool off.
                     He'll be back soon.

In saying this line as a performer playing Sheila you may speed up the delivery ✓ because the line is said hastily to reassure the Inspector that her brother Eric will be back to answer questions later ✓. Alternatively, you might suggest that there is a slightly panicked tone ✓ in the delivery to indicate that Sheila is uncertain and is merely offering a quick cover to divert attention away from her absent brother ✓.

The second question

The 6 mark question also casts you as a performer, and might look like this:

> **2(a)(ii)** You are going to play Birling. He is the head of the household and is important. As a performer, give three suggestions of how you would use performance skills from the start of the extract to the end. You must provide a reason for each suggestion. **(6 marks)**

In your response you will get one mark (✓) for each suggestion and one mark (✓) for each appropriate reason. For example:

- Use of space
- Body language
- Facial gesture
- Posture
- Eye contact
- Vocal delivery – tone, pitch, pace, pause, volume
- Gesture

You could again refer to vocal delivery, for example:

    (line 50) BIRLING: (astounded) Mrs Birling!

You could outline how you intend to say this in an indignant tone with loud volume ✓ to demonstrate how shocked you are that Eva Smith tried to pretend her surname was Birling when applying for money from the charity ✓.

You might also refer to eye contact, for example:

> (line 35) BIRLING: Is there any reason why my wife should answer questions from you, Inspector?

You could discuss how you would establish eye contact with the Inspector ✓ in order to show that you are attempting to regain status and challenge his authority while also, as the head of the family, protecting your wife ✓. For the same line you might also add how your posture would straighten ✓ as if squaring up to the Inspector ✓.

Or you might refer to facial expression, such as on the line:

> (line 42) BIRLING: Is this true?

Here you are questioning what your wife has just revealed about having met Eva recently ✓ and you might say you would furrow your brow and look at her quizzically and slightly afraid of what she has revealed ✓. You could also discuss Birling's presence in the space in relation to others in the extract ✓ to demonstrate his status in relation to the family and the Inspector ✓.

The third question

The third, fourth and fifth questions ask you to imagine you are a director and then a designer working on the play. In order to prepare for this part of the exam you must have made all the production decisions you would make if you were indeed directing or designing it: it is not enough just to have got to know the text and made character or acting decisions.

Research past productions and have in mind a set design. Choose a form of stage layout from those explained on pages 10-11 of this book. You also need to know where people might be in the room at key moments, entrances and exits, the position and style of any furniture, costumes, and so on. All decisions must be ones you know how to justify.

Context is extremely important. Make sure as part of your revision that you thoroughly research the context of both the time and place in which the play was written, and the time and place in which it is set. Try the search-term 'JB Priestley political views'. The context will form the basis for some of your answers.

Here is an example of the third question:

> **2(b)(i) As a director, discuss how you would use one of the production elements below to bring this extract to life for your audience. You should make reference to the context in which the text was created and performed. (9 marks)**
>
> Choose one of the following:
> - costume
> - staging
> - props/stage furniture

COMPONENT 3: THEATRE MAKERS IN PRACTICE

In your response, if choosing **costume**, you could refer to:

How you would use costume to indicate the time period of the piece and/or status of the characters. For example, at an Edwardian dinner party in 1912 the men are likely to be in 'tails' ✓ to show their status ✓ but also the sense of occasion ✓. The Inspector needs to stand out from the rest of the party ✓. He could, for example, wear brown in contrast to the other men assembled ✓. You could choose to use colour perhaps to indicate/symbolise something about a character. Sheila got Eva fired from Milwards because she was jealous of her. Maybe, therefore, Sheila's dress could be green ✓ to indicate her jealousy as an initial character trait ✓. Ease of use for performers could also be mentioned. As demonstrated, in each case you must justify your ideas.

In your response if choosing **staging** you could refer to:

Entrances and exits. Type of staging. Sight lines. Levels. Staging is another term for **blocking**; deliberate choices about where the performers stand and how they move on stage to communicate character relationships and plot, and to create interesting stage pictures in relation to the set, **props** and audience. In each case you must justify your ideas just as for the costume example.

In your response, if choosing **props/stage furniture** you could refer to:

Props within the space or personal props (as appropriate) to help indicate character, time period and location or symbolic meaning. In each case again you must justify your ideas, just as was shown in the costume example.

In all answers the audience should be central to the response. If you are choosing to be authentic to the time period, in this case Edwardian, research the time period and use images from the time and from past productions to help you.

The fourth question

This question also asks you to think from the perspective of a director:

> 2(b)(ii) Throughout the play the Inspector interrogates the Birling family to uncover their secrets. As a director, discuss how the performer playing this role might demonstrate his questioning techniques to the audience in this extract and the complete play. (12 marks)
>
> You must consider:
> - voice
> - physicality
> - stage directions and stage space

In your response you must show an understanding of how a director works with a performer in a specific role within the given extract, but then you should also **link** this understanding to the whole text.

For example, for the line:

    (line 5) Inspector: Mrs Birling, you're a member - a prominent member -
                of the Brumley Women's Charity Organization, aren't you?

You could discuss how the Inspector's question could be delivered with a lighter tone ✓, as if lulling Mrs Birling into a false sense of security ✓. The choice to point out she is a prominent member of the organization could be slowed – perhaps with a slight **beat** on the dash ✓ – to ensure it is clear for the audience that she had huge influence over the choices the charity made in terms of who to help ✓. For some questions the Inspector asks, you might decide he looks not at Mrs Birling, but at others in the room ✓ to see their reaction to what she reveals ✓.

It may be useful to discuss how, often, the Inspector is offering rhetorical questions and leading/loaded statements ✓. Instances of these are visually easy to spot in the first instance, because there is no question mark at the end of the lines ✓. The delivery then might indicate that the Inspector already knows the truth and knows something about what will follow on from such statements ✓. For example, when he reveals that Eva changed her name to Daisy Renton, he is dropping in information which he knows implicates another guilty party to then be interrogated – here, Gerald. When he makes this first reveal, in act one (page 25), Gerald is so taken aback by hearing the name he asks for the Inspector to repeat it. You might discuss how the Inspector delivers the line in the first place – does he already look at Gerald knowing the name will resonate with him – or is it only when he repeats the name that the inflection in his voice makes it clear he knows her name will be of significance to Gerald?

These suggestions are only a starting point, remember that you're looking to achieve 12 marks for this question and be sure to write enough.

The fifth question

You will notice that each question has carried more marks than the one before, so you must write a little more for each answer. A final 14 mark question might look like this:

> **2(c) There are specific choices in this extract for designers. Discuss how you would use one design element to enhance the production of this extract for the audience. (14 marks)**
>
> Choose one of the following:
> - Set
> - Lighting
> - Sound

If you choose **sound** as your design element, for example, you need to discuss whether you would have live or recorded sound (or a mix of both) and whether you would use music. You need to justify your choices and give specific examples, such as: to create atmosphere ✓, a ticking clock ✓ could underscore and build ✓ at moments when Mrs Birling is not immediate in her answers, to increase the tension of the pause ✓.

If you have prepared the text thoroughly and imagined yourself in the role of director and of designer as well as an actor playing the various characters, you will be well equipped to give imaginative answers: just remember that you must **justify** every decision you make.

> The stage layout and design pages of this book can help you in your decisions. Turn to pages 10-11 and 156-171. Researching previous productions is also an excellent source of inspiration.

The Crucible
by Arthur Miller

The context of the play

In 1692, several girls in a town called Salem in Massachusetts fell ill, suffering from hallucinations and seizures. No one could explain the sickness, and because the community in New England at the time was a very devout Puritan one, people attributed it to the devil.

Some of the girls began to accuse other members of the community of being witches: working with the devil and casting spells against them. Hysteria spread, and many people with old grudges against others over personal slights or claims to land began to wade in to the accusations. The system of law, which was also built on religious foundations, tried and condemned nineteen people and two dogs to death by hanging.

Arthur Miller was inspired to write his play in the early 1950s, also in the United States, by the actions of Senator Joseph McCarthy. During the Cold War there was a great fear of Communism, and McCarthy sought out communist sympathisers in America by conducting investigations in which people were encouraged to escape punishment by identifying others. Many did so in spite of their own and others' innocence, as the fear and hysteria grew. Miller saw what was happening and saw parallels with the true story of 'the Salem witch-hunts'. He wrote his play as a reminder of how such an unjust situation could get out of hand.

A plot summary

1692, Salem, Massachusetts. The Reverend Parris catches a group of girls including his daughter Betty and niece Abigail, dancing in the forest with Tituba, a black slave. The next day Betty Parris lies seriously ill and dark rumours begin to circulate. The Reverend Hale, an expert on witchcraft, is summoned.

Betty wakes screaming and Reverend Hale begins to question Abigail: flustered by his questions, she blames Tituba for bewitching her. Tituba is sent for, she is quickly confused and agrees to any suggestion that is put to her, ultimately admitting to associating with the devil. Abigail joins Tituba and they begin to list townspeople that they have seen with the devil.

Eight days later Elizabeth and John Proctor are discussing the trials and the alarming number of accused townspeople. Elizabeth pleads with John to condemn Abigail who she believes to be behind the false accusations and with whom Proctor has committed adultery.

Mary Warren, one of Abigail's friends and the Proctors' servant, returns from her duties in the court. She tells them that Elizabeth has been accused of witchcraft but the accusation is not being followed up. Giles Corey and Francis Nurse come to the Proctors' with the news that their wives have been arrested, and soon after Reverend Hale arrives and questions John about his absence from church. Later, Herrick arrives to arrest Elizabeth.

The next day Mary agrees to testify against Abigail but when Mary reveals in court that the girls are lying they accuse Mary of using witchcraft to attack them. Furious, Proctor admits his affair with Abigail. Abigail and the girls continue pretending that Mary is bewitching them which leads to Mary accusing Proctor of being a witch.

Months pass and the unrest caused by the trials has spread. On the morning of his execution Proctor is given the chance to confess rather than hang. He reluctantly agrees but when he finds out that the confession must be made public he refuses to tarnish his good name and is sent to the gallows.

John Proctor and Mary Warren in *The Crucible*, Regents Park Open Air Theatre, 2010

The characters

JOHN PROCTOR is a local farmer and generally a good man. However, it is revealed that he has had an affair with his servant Abigail. Proctor can see through people's motives for their accusations of witchcraft and he is portrayed as an honest character. Proctor is reluctant to speak out against Abigail but in the end he has no choice and is forced to reveal his infidelity. Proctor refuses to ruin his good name by making a public confession to witchcraft and is executed.

ELIZABETH PROCTOR is a loyal wife but a cold woman. She is true to her faith and is deeply hurt by Proctor's affair with Abigail; Proctor feels that Elizabeth is unforgiving. She is devoted to her husband and when asked to confirm his confession of adultery in court, Elizabeth goes against her faith and what her husband expects, and lies to protect him. This becomes Proctor's downfall. When Proctor is given the opportunity to make a false confession to save himself, Elizabeth supports his choice to be true to himself, even if it means the gallows.

ABIGAIL WILLIAMS is the seventeen year old orphaned niece of Reverend Parris and leader of the girls caught dancing in the forest. Abigail was a servant in the Proctor's house but was dismissed when Elizabeth discovered the affair. Abigail still has feelings for Proctor and wants revenge on Elizabeth, she is intelligent and manipulative: she performs convincingly in the court room and people believe her false testimony. Abigail is happy to condemn anyone she can and doesn't care about the consequences.

COMPONENT 3: THEATRE MAKERS IN PRACTICE

REVEREND PARRIS is the local clergyman and father of Betty. It is Parris who finds the girls dancing in the forest.

BETTY PARRIS is Reverend Parris' ten year old daughter and only child. She falls into a trance after being caught dancing in the forest. The mysterious illness of Betty and **RUTH PUTNAM** begins the rumours about witchcraft.

THOMAS PUTNAM is a wealthy man who uses the trials as a way of buying land to increase his wealth.

ANN PUTNAM is convinced that supernatural forces had something to do with the death of her seven babies. Ruth is her only surviving child.

MERCY LEWIS is the Putnams' servant and one of Abigail's group.

MARY WARREN works for the Proctors but is a friend of Abigail. She is shy, excitable and easily manipulated by Abigail. She agrees to testify against Abigail but is not strong enough to stand up to her in court.

TITUBA is a black slave from Barbados who works for the Parrises. In the forest she shows the girls some spells and dancing. When questioned she becomes terrified and would confess to anything.

REVEREND HALE is summoned to Salem as an expert on witchcraft and he is enthusiastic in his approach to revealing the witches.

DEPUTY-GOVERNOR DANFORTH is the powerful man in charge of the trial.

JUDGE HATHORNE is a harsh man, he believes anyone protesting against the trials must be guilty.

HERRICK is the court officer.

CHEEVER is the clerk of the court.

Sample questions

As well as the question paper, you will get a source booklet with the extracts from each of the set texts on offer. You will only have studied one text, so find the extract you need in the source booklet and don't worry about the rest. The extract will be roughly 3 pages long in the source booklet and will link to roughly 4 pages from the copy of the text you are recommended to use in class.

In the question paper, the first line will say:

'You are involved in staging a production of this play. Please read the extract on page X of the source booklet.'

Look over the extract, which should be familiar to you from your study in class and your revision. Then begin to respond to the questions. It is recommended that you spend an hour on this section of the exam.

Remember: you are responding as a performer, director or designer. This is not English literature – it's Drama.

The sample questions on the next few pages relate to the following extract from pages 18-22 of the prescribed Methuen edition of *The Crucible*. You will need to apply the suggestions made for the sample questions to the extract and questions you are given. If your preparation and understanding is good enough, it makes no difference whether you have practised the exact questions or not, you will be able to adapt.

ABIGAIL: *(with hushed trepidation)* How is Ruth sick?

MERCY: It's weirdish, I know not – she seems to walk like a dead one since last night.

ABIGAIL: *(turns at once and goes to BETTY, and now, with fear in her voice)* Betty? *(BETTY doesn't move. She shakes her.)* Now stop this! Betty! Sit up now!

BETTY doesn't stir. MERCY comes over.

MERCY: Have you tried beatin' her? I gave Ruth a good one and it waked her for a minute. Here, let me have her.

ABIGAIL: *(holding MERCY back)* No, he'll be comin' up. Listen, now; if they be questioning us, tell them we danced – I told him as much already.

MERCY: Aye. And what more?

ABIGAIL: He knows Tituba conjured Ruth's sisters to come out of the grave.

MERCY: And what more?

ABIGAIL: He saw you naked.

MERCY: *(clapping her hands together with a frightened laugh)* Oh, Jesus!

Enter MARY WARREN, breathless. She is seventeen, a subservient, naive, lonely girl.

MARY WARREN: What'll we do? The village is out! I just come from the farm; the whole country's talkin' witchcraft! They'll be callin' us witches, Abby!

MERCY: *(pointing and looking at MARY WARREN)* She means to tell, I know it.

MARY WARREN: Abby, we've got to tell. Witchery's a hangin' error, a hangin' like they done in Boston two year ago! We must tell the truth, Abby! You'll only be whipped for dancin', and the other things!

ABIGAIL: Oh, *we'll* be whipped!

MARY WARREN: I never done none of it, Abby. I only looked!

MERCY: *(moving menacingly toward MARY)* Oh, you're a great one for lookin', aren't you, Mary Warren? What a grand peeping courage you have!

BETTY, on the bed, whimpers. ABIGAIL turns to her at once.

ABIGAIL: Betty? *(She goes to BETTY)* Now, Betty, dear, wake up now. It's Abigail. *(She sits BETTY up and furiously shakes her.)* I'll beat you, Betty! *(BETTY whimpers.)* My, you seem improving. I talked to your papa and I told him everything. So there's nothing to –

BETTY: *(darts off the bed, frightened of ABIGAIL, and flattens herself against the wall)* I want my mama!

ABIGAIL: *(with alarm, as she cautiously approaches BETTY)* What ails you, Betty? Your mama's dead and buried.

BETTY: I'll fly to Mama. Let me fly! *(She raises her arms as though to fly, and streaks for the window, gets one leg out.)*

ABIGAIL: *(pulling her away from the window)* I told him everything; he knows now, he knows everything we — 40

BETTY: You drank blood, Abby! You didn't tell him that!

ABIGAIL: Betty, you never say that again! You will never—

BETTY: You did, you did! You drank a charm to kill John Proctor's wife! You drank a charm to kill Goody Proctor!

ABIGAIL: *(smashes her across the face)* Shut it! Now shut it! 45

BETTY: *(collapsing on the bed)* Mama, Mama! *(She dissolves into sobs.)*

ABIGAIL: Now look you. All of you. We danced. And Tituba conjured Ruth Putnam's dead sisters. And that is all. And mark this. Let either of you breathe a word, or the edge of a word, about the other things, and I will come to you in the black 50 of some terrible night and I will bring a pointy reckoning that will shudder you. And you know I can do it; I saw Indians smash my dear parents' heads on the pillow next to mine, and I have seen some reddish work done at night, and I can make you wish you had never seen the sun go down! *(She goes* 55 *to BETTY and roughly sits her up.)* Now, you — sit up and stop this! *(But Betty collapses in her hands and lies inert on the bed.)*

MARY WARREN: *(with hysterical fright)* What's got her? *(ABIGAIL stares in fright at BETTY.)* Abby, she's going to die! It's a sin to conjure, and we — 60

ABIGAIL: *(starting for MARY)* I say shut it, Mary Warren!

Enter JOHN PROCTOR. On seeing him, MARY WARREN leaps in fright.

MARY WARREN: Oh! I'm just going home, Mr. Proctor.

PROCTOR: Be you foolish, Mary Warren? Be you deaf? I forbid you leave the house, did I not? Why shall I pay you? I am looking for you more often than my cows! 65

MARY WARREN: I only come to see the great doings in the world.

PROCTOR: I'll show you a great doin' on your arse one of these days. Now get you home; my wife is waitin' with your work! *(Trying to retain a shred of dignity, she goes slowly out.)*

MERCY: *(both afraid of him and strangely titillated)* I'd best be off. I have my Ruth to watch. Good morning, Mr. Proctor. 70

MERCY sidles out. Since PROCTOR's entrance, ABIGAIL has stood as though on tiptoe, absorbing his presence, wide-eyed. He glances at her, then goes to BETTY on the bed.

ABIGAIL: Gah! I'd almost forgot how strong you are, John Proctor!

PROCTOR: *(looking at ABIGAIL now, the faintest suggestion of a knowing smile on his face)* What's this mischief here?

ABIGAIL: *(with a nervous laugh)* Oh, she's only gone silly somehow.

```
PROCTOR: The road past my house is a pilgrimage to Salem all
    morning. The town's mumbling witchcraft.                        75
ABIGAIL: Oh, pish! (Winningly she comes a little closer, with
    a confidential, wicked air) We were dancin' in the woods last
    night, and my uncle leaped in on us. She took fright, is all.
PROCTOR: (his smile widening) Ah, you're wicked yet, aren't y'!
    (A trill of expectant aughter escapes her, and she dares
    come closer, feverishly looking into his eyes.) You'll be
    clapped in the stocks before you're twenty. (He takes a       80
    step to go, and she springs into his path.)
ABIGAIL: Give me a word, John. A soft word. (Her concentrated
    desire destroys his smile.)
PROCTOR: No, no, Abby. That's done with.
```

The first question

The first question requires you to imagine you are a performer in the play. A possible question might be:

4(a) There are specific choices in this extract for performers.

(i) You are going to play Mary Warren. Explain two ways you would use physical skills to play this character in this extract. (4 marks)

You will receive one mark (✓) for each way identified and one mark (✓) for your explanation so it is important that you not only explain what physical skill you would use but why you would use it. Here are some ideas, but you wouldn't need them all – it's only a 4 mark question.

You could think about **movement** and **gestures**. Mary is breathless when she enters the room. You might bend forward and breathe deeply indicating that Mary has run all the way ✓. This shows that she is keen to find out what is happening to Betty and to the others who were in the woods ✓.

On the line

(line 17) MARY WARREN: What'll we do... They'll be callin' us witches Abby!

you might raise your hands to your face in fear and anxiety ✓, because you know what has happened to witches in other places ✓.

Or you could look at the moment after Abigail says

ABIGAIL: Oh, *we'll* be whipped!

MARY WARREN: I never done none of it, Abby. I only looked!

You might rush towards her on your line ✓. You could grab hold of her arm or hand ✓ in a desperate attempt to get Abigail to excuse you from your involvement ✓.

When Mercy moves menacingly towards you in line 28, you might step backwards, perhaps holding your arms in front of you to keep Mercy away or wrapping them around yourself to protect you ✓. These movements will show your fear; not only of what Mercy or Abigail might do but of the whole situation which is very serious ✓.

During the exchange between Abigail and Betty, Mary is terrified. You might watch in wide eyed horror perhaps with your hands to your face or covering your mouth ✓. You might be wringing your hands to show your anxiety ✓.

When Abigail says

(line 61) ABIGAIL: *(starting for MARY)* I say shut it, Mary Warren!

you might push yourself into a corner or against a wall ✓ to try to keep yourself as far away from the action as possible ✓. Consider how you might try to make yourself as small as possible to hide from what is happening. At this point you are hysterical with fright. Remember that the fear you feel is not just the fear from the room but the fear of what is happening in the town.

The second question

The 6 mark question also casts you as a performer, and might look like this:

> **4(a)(ii) You are going to play Mercy Lewis. As a performer, give three suggestions of how you would use performance skills from the start of the extract to the end. (6 marks)**

When Mercy enters she is keen to share what has happened to Ruth with Abigail. Her voice might be low in volume ✓ as Betty is sick ✓, but fast paced ✓ to suggest the urgency of the situation ✓.

When Abigail reveals that Parris saw you naked in the forest, you clap your hands together with a frightened laugh because you are embarrassed and scared. When you say

(line 16) MERCY: *(clapping her hands together with a frightened laugh)*
     Oh, Jesus!

it might be slowly with genuine fear that you were seen ✓ or perhaps nervous laughter and embarrassment might be in your voice when you speak ✓.

Mary Warren's frightened entrance into the room changes the atmosphere. You are immediately worried that she is going to reveal the truth. When she enters you might glare at her with hard, narrowed eyes ✓. After her first line you point directly at her and might use a harsh, demanding tone ✓ when you say

(line 20) MERCY: *(pointing and looking at MARY WARREN)* She means to tell,
     I know it.

When Mary claims that she only watched in the woods, Mercy feels angry that Mary is trying to blame the others. She moves menacingly towards her and might use fast paced, emphatic tone ✓ when she says

(line 28) MERCY: *(moving menacingly toward MARY)* Oh, you're a great
     one for lookin', aren't you, Mary Warren?

She might hold eye contact with Mary as she moves towards her ✓. She might walk slowly to add menace to her movement ✓.

The exchange between Betty and Abigail is frightening for everyone. Betty reveals exactly what happened when she says

```
(line 43) BETTY: ...You drank a charm to kill John Proctor's wife!
                 You drank a charm to kill Goody Proctor!
```

You might lose your brave face, you could put your hands to your face and gasp loudly at Betty's words ✓. Despite being angry at Mary you might move towards her for support ✓. When Abigail attacks Betty and *smashes her across the face* you would be visibly distressed. You might shake, wrap your arms around yourself or wring your hands ✓ to show that you are afraid of Abigail and the situation ✓

When John Proctor enters the room all of the girls regain their composure. You might wipe at your eyes or nose and adjust your headscarf to tidy yourself up ✓. You might feel embarrassed when Proctor tells Mary

```
(line 67) PROCTOR: I'll show you a great doin' on your arse one of these days.
```

as you too should be working ✓. You might lower your eyes and turn away from him, crossing your arms over your chest ✓. As you speak to him you might look at him through lowered eyes and smile slightly ✓ as although you are afraid of his authority you're also *strangely titillated* by him ✓.

The third question

The third, fourth and fifth questions ask you to imagine you are a director and then a designer working on the play. In order to prepare for this part of the exam you must have made all the production decisions you would make if you were indeed directing or designing it: it is not enough just to have got to know the text and made character or acting decisions.

Research past productions and have in mind a set design. Choose a form of stage layout from those explained on pages 10-11 of this book. You also need to know where people might be in the room at key moments, entrances and exits, the position and style of any furniture, costumes, and so on. All decisions must be ones you know how to justify.

Context is extremely important. Make sure as part of your revision that you thoroughly research the context of both the time and place in which the play was written, and the time and place in which it is set. Try the search term 'Salem witch hunts'. The context will form the basis for some of your answers.

Here is an example of the third question:

4(b)(i) As a director, discuss how you would use one of the production elements below to bring this extract to life for your audience. You should make reference to the context in which the text was created and performed. (9 marks)

Chose one of the following:
- Costume
- Staging
- Props/stage furniture

The girls see visions in the court. Regents Park Open Air Theatre, 2010

If you choose costume:

The girls of the time would have worn a long shirt or shift with a long dress or skirt and a fitted jacket on top. They often wore an apron and usually a bonnet to cover their hair which would have been tied back or in a bun. Aprons and bonnets were often white. Men wore breeches (short trousers) with stockings and a shirt. Over the top they would have worn a loose fitting jacket called a doublet. Men would have worn wide brimmed black or brown hats. Black leather boots or shoes were common for both men and women. Contrary to popular belief, the Puritans did not dress only in black, clothes would have been dyed with vegetable dyes so costumes might be brown, green or grey. However, they would have been quite plain, simple and practical. Betty is ill in bed so would be wearing modest nightclothes: a long, ankle length nightgown would be appropriate.

If you choose staging:

For this element you must consider the type of stage you would use. You might opt for the traditional **proscenium arch** staging which would give you the opportunity to use a backdrop to set the room using things such as the bedroom wall and window.

The initial focus of this scene before the beginning of the extract is Betty's illness, so it might be appropriate for her bed to be **centre stage** with Abigail positioned **stage left** watching over Betty.

However, in this extract Abigail dominates the other girls and Proctor, so she might command most of the stage left while the other girls are positioned **stage right** close to the door. The exchange between Proctor and Abigail could take place **downstage centre**, close to the audience to allow them to see the relationship between the pair.

If you choose props/stage furniture:

You might decide to make the setting of the stage very naturalistic, which would offer opportunities for different props to create Betty's bedroom. It's important to remember that it would have been plain and simple but could include the bed, a chair, drawers, the window and props such as a water jug, a bible and a crucifix: all of this shows your understanding of the **context**.

The fourth question

This question also asks you to think from the perspective of a director:

> **4(b)(ii)** Abigail is the play's female protagonist. As a director, discuss how the performer playing this role might demonstrate her power in this extract and the complete play. **(12 marks)**
>
> You must consider:
> - Voice
> - Physicality
> - Stage directions and stage space

In your response you must show an understanding of how a director works with a performer in a specific role within the given extract, but then you should also **link** this understanding to the whole text.

In this extract a performer playing the role of Abigail could use a variety of vocal skills to show their power. Abigail is the person who answers Mercy and Mary's questions. When she says lines such as *'Now stop this!'* (to Betty) *'Listen now'* (to Mercy) and *'Oh, we'll be whipped!'* (to Mary) she might have a loud, strong and commanding voice with a low, deep tone ✓ giving no doubt as to who is in charge of the situation ✓.

In each of these moments she could move physically closer to the person she is addressing: she shakes Betty ✓, she holds Mercy back when she approaches Betty ✓ and gestures towards the whole group when telling Mary that they will all be whipped ✓, perhaps raising an eyebrow and with a cynical smile ✓.

During her speech *'Now look you. All of you... I can make you wish you'd never seen the sun go down,* her pace could be fast with a lower pitch as she becomes angry ✓, she might be especially forceful on words such as *'either of you'*, *'breathe a word'*, *'pointy reckoning'*, *'smash'* and *'reddish work'* ✓. The volume might increase as her tone becomes harsher ✓, she might grit her teeth or hiss some of her words ✓.

With this extract she might stand centre stage as she directs her words at the girls ✓. She might use large gestures with her arms and clench her fists when she talks about her parents ✓. She could breathe heavily and have wild, open eyes ✓.

In contrast to this, Abigail's tone is much softer and higher pitched when she addresses Proctor ✓. She is *wide eyed* when he enters and has a light, flirtatious tone when she says *'I'd almost forgot how strong you are, John Proctor!'* and laughs nervously around him ✓ showing us that she is weakened by him and still has feelings for him ✓. Her voice might become more urgent and faster paced as she pleads with him *'Give me a word, John. A soft word.'* ✓

She would move physically closer to him, *with a confidential, wicked air,* and perhaps reach out a hand towards him ✓. She might use a flirtatious gesture such as twirling her hair or look longingly at him ✓. She might raise her hands to her mouth as she laughs nervously ✓.

COMPONENT 3: THEATRE MAKERS IN PRACTICE

Later in the play, in act 3 (page 98) we see further evidence of Abigail's power when she is questioned in court by Danforth, in her response *'I have been hurt, Mr Danforth... To be mistrusted, denied, questioned like a –'*. Here she could show her power by using a high pitched, tearful, childlike voice with a low volume ✓ to make Danforth feel guilty for his question as we see him *weakening* ✓. Here Abigail might try to use a childlike posture by crossing her arms and fidgeting her feet, she might use eye contact hesitantly to show she is upset ✓.

This contrasts with her next statement which would be louder, firmer, lower pitched and faster paced when she uses an *open threat*: *'Let you beware, Mr Danforth.'* ✓ Abigail would show her power physically by standing straight with rigid shoulders, she would glare at Danforth and perhaps go as far as to point a finger at him ✓. Her power is further reinforced when she pretends that Mary is bewitching her.

The fifth question

You will notice that each question has carried more marks than the one before, so you must write a little more for each answer. A final 14 mark question might look like this:

> **4(c) There are specific choices in this extract for designers. Discuss how you would use one design element to enhance the production of this extract for the audience. (14 marks)**
>
> Choose one of the following:
> - Set
> - Lighting
> - Sound

In answering this question it is important that you show your ability to use appropriate technical language and justify how your choices would enhance the extract for the audience.

If you choose lighting, for example, you might choose to light the scene with a warm wash ✓ as it's inside a house on a cold day ✓. The lighting might become colder and harsher as Abigail begins her warning to the girls ✓ or perhaps the use of a coloured light might enhance her speech ✓, snapping back to a warm wash as she says *'I can make you wish you had never seen the sun go down. Now, you – sit up and stop this!'* ✓.

If you choose sound, you might include the sounds of the people gathering downstairs in the Parris house ✓. Before he exits Reverend Parris says he will lead the crowd in a psalm so you might include the sound of his voice and murmuring of the others praying ✓. Perhaps there is the sound from outside of birds or running water to suggest a rural setting ✓.

> **The stage layout and design pages of this book can help you in your decisions. Turn to pages 10-11 and 156-171. Researching previous productions is also an excellent source of inspiration.**

Government Inspector
by Nikolai Gogol
(adapted by David Harrower)

The context of the play

Living in Russia under Tsar Nicholas I, in 1835 Gogol wrote to his friend Alexander Pushkin asking for an anecdote on which he could base a comedy play, and in 1836 *Government Inspector* was published.

It is a **satire** about people's greed and stupidity, and highlights the political corruption which Gogol saw around him in Imperial Russia.

A plot summary

In a small, provincial town in Russia the Mayor announces to his officials that a government inspector is visiting, most likely incognito. The corrupt officials are thrown into a panic: worried that their dishonesty will be exposed, the group determine to hide their corruption, and speedily clean up the town.

Bobchinsky and Dobchinsky, two local landowners, arrive at the Mayor's office with news that a mysterious stranger has been staying at the local inn. Everyone is convinced that he must be the inspector. The Mayor prepares himself and heads out to welcome him.

In the local inn, Khlestakov, a lowly civil servant, is broke after gambling his money away playing cards. He and his servant Osip haven't eaten for days and the innkeeper is refusing to serve them any more food until the bill is settled. The Mayor, believing that Khlestakov is the government inspector, arrives and insists that he comes and stays at his home. Khlestakov is confused and surprised by the Mayor's offer but readily accepts his kindness.

Meanwhile, when Anna and Maria, the Mayor's wife and daughter, hear that the inspector is coming to stay they question Dobchinsky about him and debate what they are going to wear. The Mayor arrives with Khlestakov and some of the other town officials. Everyone compliments Khlestakov and he begins to invent more and more outrageous stories about his life achievements.

The next day Khlestakov meets with many of the officials, all of whom offer him money which he happily accepts. He writes a letter to a friend which describes the mistaken identity and mocks the townspeople. He meets with a range of disgruntled shopkeepers eager to tell their stories about the Mayor's unscrupulous running of the town; and he receives more money as he listens to their woes and promises to resolve their problems.

Khlestakov seduces Maria and asks for her hand in marriage. Maria accepts and the Mayor is delighted by what he imagines will be his imminent elevated status. Meanwhile, Osip realises he and Khlestakov will soon be caught out and organises a horse and carriage for them to leave. Khlestakov says he's going to his uncle's estate to share the happy news and accepts another handful of money from the Mayor.

Alistair McGowan plays Khlestakov at the Chichester Festival Theatre, 2005

Anna and Maria daydream about St. Petersburg life as the officials arrive to offer their congratulations. As the Mayor brags about his good fortune the Postmaster arrives with Khlestakov's letter which he has intercepted. Khlestakov is exposed as an impostor and the officials furiously try to blame each other for the mistake. They all conclude that the fault lies with Dobchinsky and Bobchinsky. While the officials rant, a policeman arrives with a letter announcing that the government inspector has arrived and everyone must report to the inn.

The characters

KHLESTAKOV is a very low ranking clerk of very little importance. He has lost all of his money gambling and is unable to pay his bill at the inn. When the Mayor arrives he believes that he is going to be arrested, but realising that he is being treated as an honoured guest, he makes the most of the error. He spins ridiculous tales, flirts outrageously with the Mayor's wife and proposes marriage to his daughter. Although Khlestakov lies, he is not deliberately dishonest to begin with, he is an opportunist who makes the most of the case of mistaken identity.

OSIP is Khlestakov's servant. We learn Khlestakov's circumstances from Osip's speeches. Osip sees what is happening much sooner than Khlestakov and gives the impression of being brighter than his master. He makes the most of the situation himself, telling the Mayor that Khlestakov is always happiest when Osip is well looked after.

THE MAYOR is in charge of the town and has the most to lose from the inspector discovering his corruption and the lazy way he has been letting the town run. Delighted by Khlestakov's acceptance of his hospitality and offers of money, and beside himself when Khlestakov proposes to his daughter – enjoying fantasies of an extravagant life in St. Petersburg, he is crushed and outraged by the revelation that Khlestakov is an imposter and that the real inspector has arrived.

ANNA the mayor's wife is vain and self-absorbed. She is in constant competition with her daughter, arguing over who Khlestakov notices most. She flirts inappropriately with Khlestakov and although she agrees to his proposal to Maria she is open about what she will gain from it.

MARIA the mayor's daughter is vain like her mother and competes for attention in the same way. Although she tries initially to reject Khlestakov's physical advances, it is not long before she surrenders.

DOBCHINSKY and BOBCHINSKY are bumbling landowners, the first to suggest that Khlestakov is the incognito inspector. They scurry around trying to make an impression and are delighted finally to have something of consequence to tell the Mayor about.

LYAPKIN-TYAPKIN is the judge, with a passion for hunting with dogs.

ZEMLYANIKA is a trustee of charitable institutions and runs the hospital, badly.

KHLOPOV is the schools superintendent. He spends much of his time terrified about the idea of the inspector and what might happen. When he finally meets with Khlestakov he can barely contain his dread.

DR GIBNER works at the hospital. He doesn't speak or understand any Russian.

MISHKA is the mayor's servant

POSTMASTER is portrayed as quite unwise. He frequently opens and reads the town's post often keeping letters that he likes.

Other characters: Police Superintendent, Avdotya, policemen, Locksmith's wife, Sergeant's widow, waiter, shopkeepers

Sample questions

As well as the question paper, you will get a source booklet with the extracts from each of the set texts on offer. You will only have studied one text, so find the extract you need in the source booklet and don't worry about the rest. The extract will be roughly 3 pages long in the source booklet and will link to roughly 4 pages from the copy of the text you are recommended to use in class.

In the question paper, the first line will say:

'You are involved in staging a production of this play. Please read the extract on page X of the source booklet.'

Look over the extract, which should be familiar to you from your study in class and your revision. Then begin to respond to the questions. It is recommended that you spend an hour on this section of the exam.

Remember: you are responding as a performer, director or designer. This is not English literature – it's Drama.

The sample questions on the next few pages relate to the following extract from pages 34-36 of the prescribed Faber & Faber edition of *Government Inspector*. You will need to apply the suggestions made for the sample questions to the extract and questions you are given. If your preparation and understanding is good enough, it makes no difference whether you have practised the exact questions or not, you will be able to adapt.

OSIP *and the WAITER arrive carrying plates.*
OSIP: Lunch…
KHLESTAKOV: Lunch?
OSIP: Lunch.
KHLESTAKOV: Lunch! What kind of lunch?
OSIP: Soup. 5
KHLESTAKOV: Soup! *(To WAITER.)* More lunch?
WAITER: Beef.
KHLESTAKOV: Beef! Beef and soup!
WAITER: Absolutely the very last time he says.
KHLESTAKOV: Who cares what he says? Bugger him. Soup and beef 10
 and… Only two courses?
WAITER: 'Fraid so. Soup. Beef.
KHLESTAKOV: *(Inspects them.)* Hang on, hang on… This isn't two courses.
WAITER: That's two courses.
KHLESTAKOV: There's nothing on these plates. 15
WAITER: Landlord says there's plenty there.
KHLESTAKOV: There's no gravy.
WAITER: You're right, there's not.
KHLESTAKOV: Yes, but when I was passing the kitchen this morning
 I saw that heartless cook you employ stirring a huge pot of 20
 gravy…Bastard saw me and licked the spoon. *And* I saw salmon!
 Why don't I get salmon? I saw two little fat men in the
 restaurant filling their fat guts with fresh salmon. How come
 those twatbags get salmon and I get this shit?
WAITER: I think you'll find they paid for it, sir. 25
KHLESTAKOV: That's the provinces all over. Feed the undeserving,
 leave the rest to rot. Unbelievable. What kind of soup is this?
WAITER: Cook didn't say, sir.
KHLESTAKOV: Didn't say or *wouldn't* say? Eugh. It is completely
 without taste. Grease, yes – uh, my teeth are coated in it… 30
 And bits of…don't know what…Euh…it gets worse, the lower it
 goes…It's dishwater, isn't it?
 Someone's washed dishes in this. *(Sniffs it, retches.)*
 It's coming back up. Osip…!
 OSIP *holds out the soup plate.* KHLESTAKOV *opens his mouth but
 catches it, swallows it down again.*
 I can't eat this. Get me something else. 35
 WAITER *attempts to remove the plate.*
 Ah ah ah! Did I say take it away? You want to watch yourself.
 My opinion of you is plummeting. You wouldn't last a second in
 Petersburg with your attitude. *(Eats.)* Euh…It's rank…Aww, look,

there's a feather in it…No no no…Give me the beef – quick,
quick…I need to get rid of this taste. Osip, you finish this. 40
(Tries to cut the beef.) It won't cut. Why won't it cut? It's
not the knife. What is this?

WAITER: Roast beef.

KHLESTAKOV: Listen, I know my beef – this is not beef. This is…
(Hacks at it with knife.) This needs a saw. An axe. This cow's 45
been dug up. Exhumed. There. Done it. *(Into mouth, chews it.)*
My jaw – you've broken my jaw! It's like wood, it splinters
in your mouth, it's like needles. My gums are lacerated.
I can taste blood. I'm internally bleeding…Ah…
(He's done, his plate's empty.)

WAITER: You done? 50

KHLESTAKOV: Is there any more? Nothing to finish with?

WAITER: 'Fraid not.

KHLESTAKOV: You know nothing about fine dining! There should always
be a dessert. It's about balance. I've such a sweet tooth…
Surely you could rustle up a sweet flaky pastry? What about 55
an Apricot Victoria? Or a Sour Cheery Flummery? An Apple
Chatelaine? Pineapple Parfait Florida? A Peach Salambo?
The WAITER leaves with the plates.
(To OSIP*)* Go after him! Follow him. Praise him! Get me more
of that beef…It was rank but I want more, I need more,
get me more… 60
OSIP *exits, then hurtles back into the room.*

OSIP: He's outside.

KHLESTAKOV: Who?

OSIP: The Mayor, the Governor, the Boss, the Top Man…

KHLESTAKOV: Oh shit. Oh no. Hide! No, I can't hide…Fine. Let him
in. They can throw me in prison but they won't break my spirit. 65
(Shouts.) You hear? I'm ready. Take me away. *(Holds his
hands out to be handcuffed. Then suddenly cowers.)* No no, I
don't want to go…Osip, Osip, help me, save me. Not prison, no,
I don't want to go to prison, don't let them…Who do they think
I am? A Serf? Go and tell him. No, I'll tell him! I'll tell 70
him to his face. How dare he even…
The doorhandle turns. KHLESTAKOV shrinks back.

COMPONENT 3: THEATRE MAKERS IN PRACTICE

The first question

The first question requires you to imagine you are a performer in the play. A possible question might be:

> **7(a) There are specific choices in this extract for performers.**
>
> (i) You are going to play Osip. Explain two ways you would use physical skills to play this character in this extract. (4 marks)

You will receive one mark (✓) for each way identified and one mark (✓) for your explanation so it is important that you not only explain **what** physical skill you would use but **why** you would use it. Here are some ideas, but you wouldn't need them all – it's only a 4 mark question.

You could think about **movement** and **gestures**. When Osip enters the room he is carrying some food. You could hold the bowl carefully and walk cautiously towards the table ✓ so as not to spill the soup ✓. When Khlestakov asks *'What kind of lunch?'* you might point to the bowl and raise your eyebrows as you reply *'Soup'* ✓ to indicate that you think it's quite obvious what it is ✓.

As Khlestakov eats you might take a step back ✓ so that you are behind him and he won't see you jealously glaring at him as he gets to eat and you don't ✓, you might hold your own stomach and look longingly at his back ✓. You might cross your arms and look at him with disgust as he wolfs the food down ✓. When he retches and says

        (line 34) KHLESTAKOV:… It's coming back up! Osip…!

you might hold the soup bowl out quite casually and turn away slightly ✓ to show that you don't appreciate the indignity of holding a bowl for him to be sick into ✓.

When Khlestakov sends you to follow the waiter you might stamp out ✓ to show that you are unhappy about it ✓ Your behaviour changes immediately however as you rush back in and say 'He's outside.' While Khlestakov panics you might show your anxiety ✓ by running your hands through your hair or putting your hands to your face ✓.

The second question

The 6 mark question also casts you as a performer, and might look like this:

> **7(a)(ii) You are going to play the waiter. As a performer, give three suggestions of how you would use performance skills from the start of the extract to the end. (6 marks)**

In this scene you are doing your job as a waiter which is to serve the guest, but you are also aware that Khlestakov has not paid his bill and that the landlord is unhappy. When you enter you might place the plate on the table and step away, standing respectfully, upright with your hands behind your back ✓ waiting for any instructions ✓. You have to be respectful to your guest but when Khlestakov questions the food you might use a resigned tone with quite a slow pace when you say *"Fraid so. Soup. Beef.'* ✓ to show that the landlord is unhappy and that there will be nothing else ✓.

The waiter might begin to feel impatient with Khlestakov's complaining ✓ so you use a slightly sarcastic tone when you say

(line 18) WAITER: You're right, there's not.

As he begins to complain about what he saw other guests eating and gets angry with you, you might begin to tense up ✓, perhaps this is shown in your shoulders hunching slightly or your hands beginning to clench ✓. When you say

(line 25) WAITER: I think you'll find they paid for it, sir.

You might be openly sarcastic on this line ✓.

While Khlestakov is making a fuss about the food and retching, you might show your annoyance ✓ by standing with your arms crossed, rolling your eyes and audibly sighing at his performance ✓. When he appears finished you might move quickly to remove his plate ✓ in order to leave ✓. When he continues his complaint you might return to having your hands behind your back and look up to the ceiling ✓ to indicate that you have had enough ✓. When he runs through his requests for dessert you might just openly stare blankly at him and perhaps sigh and turn away when he finishes the list ✓. You might take the plate and leave without looking back ✓ This would be considered disrespectful but at this point, you don't care ✓.

The third question

The third, fourth and fifth questions ask you to imagine you are a director and then a designer working on the play. In order to prepare for this part of the exam you must have made all the production decisions you would make if you were indeed directing or designing it: it is not enough just to have got to know the text and made character or acting decisions.

Research past productions and have in mind a set design. Choose a form of stage layout from those explained on pages 10-11 of this book. You also need to know where people might be in the room at key moments, entrances and exits, the position and style of any furniture, costumes, and so on. All decisions must be ones you know how to justify.

Context is extremely important. Make sure as part of your revision that you thoroughly research the context of both the time and place in which the play was written, and the time and place in which it is set. Try the search term 'pre-revolutionary Russia'. The context will form the basis for some of your answers.

Here is an example of the third question:

> 7(b)(i) As a director, discuss how you would use one of the production elements below to bring this extract to life for your audience. You should make reference to the context in which the text was created and performed. (9 marks)
>
> Choose one of the following:
> - Costume
> - Staging
> - Props/stage furniture

COMPONENT 3: THEATRE MAKERS IN PRACTICE

If you choose costume:

You can use your choice of costume in this scene to define the differences clearly in the status of the three characters. Khlestakov has the highest status in the scene and would be more smartly dressed than Osip and the waiter. However, Khlestakov has gambled all of his money away so perhaps his costume is showing signs of wear. He might be wearing reasonably well made trousers, a shirt, tie and waistcoat, probably without a jacket as he is in his room but perhaps the waistcoat is frayed round the edges or has buttons missing, maybe his shirt cuffs are worn to show that although he has owned nice clothes, he can't afford to replace them and looks rather dishevelled. Consider the colours that Khlestakov might wear in his tie and waistcoat. He becomes quite exaggerated and flamboyant and you might choose to express this with some colour. Think about the fashion of the time period or how you might use modern costumes.

As Khlestakov's servant, Osip might be dressed in a simple shirt, tie and trousers. He would need to look smart to represent Khlestakov but would not have the money to buy extravagant clothes.

The waiter has the lowest status and perhaps this could be shown by even more simple clothing: plain trousers and a linen shirt. He would be likely to be wearing an apron. Consider the humour in how you present the waiter, he might wear a crisp, clean uniform to contrast with Khlestakov's dishevelled appearance or he might wear a filthy, stained apron suggesting that the food in the inn is as bad as Khlestakov claims.

If you choose staging:

Staging is another term for **blocking**; deliberate choices about where the performers stand and how they move on stage to communicate character relationships and plot, and to create interesting stage pictures in relation to the set, **props** and audience. You might decide to use a **proscenium arch** for the staging of your production to keep with the original production style of the 1830s. You might however, decide to use a different stage such as a **thrust stage** with the audience on three sides. This would give the scene a more intimate feel for the audience, as if they are part of the action.

If you choose props/stage furniture:

The scene is set in the inn, in Khlestakov's room. The room might include a messy bed and items of Khlestakov's clothes strewn around to indicate his chaotic personality. A table and chairs is essential for Khlestakov to sit and eat, this should be close to the audience so that they can really see his dramatic, exaggerated facial expressions. This close proximity would be important when Khlestakov retches when eating. Remember that the play is a light hearted **farce**, so these moments of comedy are important for engaging the audience.

The fourth question

This question also asks you to think from the perspective of a director:

> **7(b)(ii)** The character of Khlestakov is often portrayed as melodramatic and exaggerated. As a director, discuss how the performer playing this role might demonstrate this in this extract and the complete play. (12 marks)
>
> You must consider:
> - Voice
> - Physicality
> - Stage directions and stage space

In your response you must show an understanding of how a director works with a performer in a specific role within the given extract, but then you should also **link** this understanding to the whole text.

At the beginning of this scene Khlestakov is quite demanding and rude to both Osip and the waiter. When he demands his lunch and complains about what he is given he might use a harsh, loud tone of voice, quite fast paced ✓ as he spits out his displeasure at the beef and soup ✓. He might screw his face up and narrow his eyes as he looks at the plates and '*inspects them*', perhaps sniffing at the food ✓ and showing his annoyance ✓. His voice might take on a higher-pitched, emphatic, whining tone ✓ as he complains

> (line 15) KHLESTAKOV: There's nothing on these plates.

As Khlestakov goes on to complain about what the paying customers were eating he might use a faster paced, angry tone ✓ as he moans about the injustice of the situation ✓. He might gesture with his arms as he talks about the men in the restaurant, perhaps pushing his stomach out and puffing out his cheeks ✓ as he says

> (line 22) KHLESTAKOV:... I saw two little fat men in the restaurant filling their fat guts with fresh salmon.

He might move very close to the waiter and take on a more childish tone and stamp his foot ✓ when he says

> (line 23) KHLESTAKOV:... How come those twatbags get salmon and I get this shit?

The part of the extract where Khlestakov is eating should take place quite close to the audience so they can see the full range of expressions that he uses. As he eats the food he could really exaggerate his facial expressions to show his revulsion, screwing up his eyes or opening them wide in horror at his meal ✓, he might point at different bits or hold it up, he '*sniffs it', retches* in close proximity to the audience ✓. His voice might switch between low and angry to high pitched and shrill with disgust ✓. He might use wide arm gestures and often put his hands to his face ✓. His disgust peaks when he threatens to be sick '*but catches it, swallows it down again'*.

When Khlestakov asks the waiter if there's any dessert he might stand **centre stage** as he lists his suggestions ✓, he might close his eyes and inhale deeply as he imagines the desserts ✓, he might move closer and closer towards the waiter using wide eyes and a hopeful, high pitched voice ✓ only to deflate as the waiter looks at him and then leaves ✓.

We see a change in Khlestakov when Osip reveals that the Mayor is here to see him. He might switch between a fast paced, high pitched voice and a low, angry tone as he frets about what is going to happen ✓. He holds his hands out to be handcuffed and then cowers and we see a range of emotions pass through him. Again he might perform in close proximity to the audience, perhaps using someone as protection ✓.

In act three, scene four we see further examples of Khlestakov's wild personality. As he moves through his tale about how important he is (page 58), how popular he is (page 59), what he has written (page 60) and his parties (page 61). In this scene there are many opportunities for Khlestakov to use large arm and hand gestures ✓, to speak with animation and use a fast paced, excited tone of voice ✓. As he addresses people he might move very close to them, in some cases, uncomfortably close as tells his stories of how magnificent he is ✓. During these speeches he would smile a lot and pace around the stage as if he is reliving the events, almost believing it is true himself ✓. As his speech continues on pages 62 and 63 he would incorporate imaginary guests, touching their arms and laughing with them ✓.

COMPONENT 3: THEATRE MAKERS IN PRACTICE

He would become louder and louder with more and more wild arm gestures until on the lines *'I am everywhere! Everywhere! Everywhere! Everywhere!'* he is perhaps standing on a chair shouting at the top of his voice ✓ when *'he slips, so caught up in his speech, and almost falls'*.

The fifth question

You will notice that each question has carried more marks than the one before, so you must write a little more for each answer. A final 14 mark question might look like this:

> **7(c) There are specific choices in this extract for designers. Discuss how you would use one design element to enhance the production of this extract for the audience. (14 marks)**
>
> Choose one of the following:
> - Set
> - Lighting
> - Sound

In answering this question it is important that you show your ability to use appropriate technical language and justify how your choices would enhance the extract for the audience.

If you choose **set**, for example, You might decide to create the room as untidy and run down, putting pictures on the wall to link to the historical period, or choose to have a curtained window that Khlestakov or Osip can peer through. Or you might consider a non-naturalistic or minimalist set using bare walls and just the table with one chair.

In this extract the **lighting** might be used to create a dim atmosphere in the room. You could use a low, cold wash to suggest that Khlestakov's room is not very inviting, this might contrast with a bright, warm wash used in the Mayor's house.

You could use the **sounds** of a busy street outside or the sounds from the inn below to enhance the scene, perhaps there is the sound of music from downstairs, this could be live or recorded. You might choose to use the sounds of a horse and carriage to signify the Mayor's arrival.

> The stage layout and design pages of this book can help you in your decisions. Turn to pages 10-11 and 156-171. Researching previous productions is also an excellent source of inspiration.

Twelfth Night
by William Shakespeare

The context of the play

Twelfth Night was written as a comedy entertainment for the end of the Christmas season, and the first recorded performance of it was not at the Globe theatre, but indoors at Middle Temple Hall, one of the London Inns of Court, on Candlemas night: 2 February 1602.

A plot summary

In the kingdom of Illyria, Duke Orsino is pining for the love of Lady Olivia. She refuses his advances because she is mourning for her dead brother.

Meanwhile, off the coast, a storm has caused a shipwreck. Viola survives but fears that her twin brother, Sebastian, has drowned. Viola disguises herself as a man and goes to work for Orsino as his page, Cesario. She quickly proves herself and becomes Orsino's favourite. Viola soon begins to fall in love with Orsino and is unhappy when he confides in her that he is in love with the mournful Olivia. Viola dutifully delivers Orsino's love messages to Olivia only for Olivia to fall in love with Viola, thinking she is a man. The love triangle is complete; Orsino loves Olivia, Olivia loves Viola (Cesario) and Viola loves Orsino.

After a late night of revelry Olivia's maid, Maria, jester, Feste, drunken uncle Sir Toby Belch, and his friend (and possible suitor for Olivia) Sir Andrew Aguecheek are all annoyed to be interrupted and sent to bed by Malvolio the head servant of the house. The revellers plot revenge and the next day send Malvolio a fake love letter from Olivia. The letter tells Malvolio that if he wants Olivia to fall in love with him he should smile constantly and dress in yellow stockings and **cross garters**. Malvolio finds the letters and falls for the trick. Olivia thinks that Malvolio has gone mad and bewildered by his behaviour she orders for him to be locked in a darkened room to recover.

In the meantime, Viola's twin, Sebastian arrives with his friend Antonio who is an old enemy of Orsino. Believing that he is competition for the hand of Olivia, Sir Andrew begins a duel with Cesario (Viola). Antonio discovers the duel and believing it to be Sebastian fighting, steps in to stop the duel. Antonio is recognised as an enemy of Orsino and arrested. When Antonio asks Viola for help (believing she is Sebastian) she refuses and he is outraged by the betrayal.

Viola leaves and, still wanting a fight, Sir Andrew and Sir Toby pursue her, but catch Sebastian. Olivia arrives and mistaking Sebastian for Viola, she rescues him. Sebastian is attracted to Olivia and she wastes no time in arranging their marriage.

Viola and Orsino arrive at Olivia's house. Olivia greets Viola as her new husband, thinking that he is Sebastian. Orsino is livid at what he thinks is a betrayal by his page. Sebastian arrives and all is revealed. The twins are reunited and Orsino, realising that Cesario is in fact Viola, asks for her hand in marriage. Malvolio is finally released from his dark room and while he storms off, the happy couples celebrate.

COMPONENT 3: THEATRE MAKERS IN PRACTICE

Viola (Cesario) and Orsino in *Twelfth Night* at the Courtyard Theatre, RSC, Stratford-upon-Avon, 2009

The characters

VIOLA is a young noblewoman who arrives in Illyria after being shipwrecked. She excels in her role as Orsino's page and soon becomes a trustworthy and loyal companion. Viola is quickly caught in a love triangle and this tricky situation dominates much of the play as we try to figure out how she will get herself out of it.

ORSINO is a powerful aristocrat in Illyria. He is in love with Olivia and mopes around complaining that she does not return his affections. Orsino becomes closer and closer to his new page and is delighted when he discovers that Cesario is in fact Viola in disguise.

OLIVIA is a beautiful and wealthy noblewoman of Illyria. She is in mourning for her dead brother and shuns the affections of both Orsino and Sir Andrew Aguecheek. She quickly changes her mind about refusing love when she falls for Cesario and is hasty to marry Sebastian when he returns her affections.

SEBASTIAN is Viola's twin brother who arrives in Illyria with Antonio. When he arrives he finds that many people think they know him and he is surprised when the beautiful Lady Olivia wants to marry him.

MALVOLIO is the conservative head servant of Olivia's house. He disapproves of the merry making and his interference in other people's fun leads to him being tricked by the fake letter that he thinks is from Olivia. He is ambitious and conceited and believes that there is a chance that Olivia will marry him, leading to his escapade in his yellow stockings.

FESTE is Olivia's fool, or jester. He sings and makes jokes, although he does offer good advice.

SIR TOBY BELCH is Olivia's uncle. He is often rowdy and drunk and enjoys playing practical jokes. He marries Olivia's maid, Maria.

SIR ANDREW AGUECHEEK is a wealthy friend of Sir Toby. He thinks he is clever and funny but he is not. Sir Andrew attempts to woo Olivia but really has no chance of success.

MARIA is Olivia's maid. She is clever and witty and enjoys the late night capers in the household. Maria forges the letter to Malvolio pretending that Olivia is in love with him.

ANTONIO rescues Sebastian from the shipwreck. He adores Sebastian and helps him financially when they arrive in Illyria.

Sample questions

As well as the question paper, you will get a source booklet with the extracts from each of the set texts on offer. You will only have studied one text, so find the extract you need in the source booklet and don't worry about the rest. The extract will be roughly 3 pages long in the source booklet and will link to roughly 4 pages from the copy of the text you are recommended to use in class.

In the question paper, the first line will say:

'You are involved in staging a production of this play. Please read the extract on page X of the source booklet.'

Look over the extract, which should be familiar to you from your study in class and your revision. Then begin to respond to the questions. It is recommended that you spend an hour on this section of the exam.

Remember: you are responding as a performer, director or designer. This is not English literature – it's Drama.

The sample questions on the next few pages relate to the following extract from pages 34-36 of the prescribed New Longman Shakespeare edition of *Twelfth Night*. You will need to apply the suggestions made for the sample questions to the extract and questions you are given. If your preparation and understanding is good enough, it makes no difference whether you have practised the exact questions or not, you will be able to adapt.

```
Act 2 scene 2
    A street.
    Enter VIOLA, MALVOLIO following.
MALVOLIO: Were not you even now with the Countess Olivia?
VIOLA: Even now, sir; on a moderate pace I have since
    arrived but hither.
MALVOLIO: She returns this ring to you, sir: you might have
    saved me my pains, to have taken it away                          5
    yourself. She adds, moreover, that you should put
    your lord into a desperate assurance she will none
    of him. And one thing more, that you be never so
    hardy to come again in his affairs, unless it be to
    report your lord's taking of this. Receive it so.                10
    He throws the ring on the ground
VIOLA: She took the ring of me: I'll none of it.
MALVOLIO: Come, sir, you peevishly threw it to her; and her
    will is, it should be so returned: if it be worth
    stooping for, there it lies in your eye; if not, be it
    his that finds it.                                               15
    Exit
VIOLA: I left no ring with her: what means this lady?
    Fortune forbid my outside hath not charm'd her!
```

COMPONENT 3: THEATRE MAKERS IN PRACTICE

```
      She made good view of me; indeed, so much
      That sure methought her eyes had lost her tongue,
      For she did speak in starts distractedly.              20
      She loves me, sure; the cunning of her passion
      Invites me in this churlish messenger.
      None of my lord's ring! Why, he sent her none.
      I am the man: if it be so, as 't is,
      Poor lady, she were better love a dream.               25
      Disguise, I see, thou art a wickedness
      Wherein the pregnant enemy does much.
      How easy is it for the proper-false
      In women's waxen hearts to set their forms!
      Alas, our frailty is the cause, not we,                30
      For such as we are made of, such we be.
      How will this fadge? My master loves her dearly;
      And I, poor monster, fond as much on him;
      And she, mistaken, seems to dote on me.
      What will become of this? As I am man,                 35
      My state is desperate for my master's love;
      As I am woman - now alas the day! -
      What thriftless sighs shall poor Olivia breathe!
      O time, thou must untangle this, not I;
      It is too hard a knot for me to untie!                 40
      Exit
```

1	**even now**	– just now
2-3	**on a moderate pace**...	– walking reasonably fast, I have only got this far.
6-7	**put your lord into**...	– make your lord certain that there is no hope that she will marry him.
9	**hardy**	– bold
11	**I'll none of it.**	– I don't want it.
12	**peevishly**	– rudely
17	**Fortune forbid my outside hath not**...	– I hope she has not been attracted by my appearance!
19-20	**methougtht her eyes had lost her tongue**...	– because she was staring at me, she couldn't speak properly
21-22	**the cunning of her passion**...	– She has used this rude messenger as a clever way of giving me an invitation.
27	**the pregnant enemy**	– the devil, full (pregnant) of cunning ideas
28-29	**How easy is it**...	– Isn't it easy for handsome but deceitful men (the proper-false) to make an impression on women's hearts.
30-31	**our frailty**...	– Our weakness is the problem: that's the way we are made.
32	**How will this fadge?**	– How will this turn out?
35-36	**As I am man**...	– While I am pretending to be a man, it is hopeless to try to win my master's love.
38	**thriftless**	– useless, profitless

The first question

The first question requires you to imagine you are a performer in the play. A possible question might be:

> **8(a) There are specific choices in this extract for performers.**
>
> (i) You are going to play Malvolio. Explain two ways you would use vocal skills to play this character in this extract. (4 marks)

Your answer will receive one mark (✓) for each way identified and one mark (✓) for your explanation so you must be able to explain not just how you would use your voice but why, showing your understanding of the character and the play. Here are some ideas, but you wouldn't need them all – it's only a 4 mark question.

For this question you might refer to **pitch**, **tone**, **pace**, **volume** or **emphasis**.

```
(line 4) MALVOLIO: She returns this ring to you, sir: you might have
                  saved me my pains, to have taken it away yourself.
```

Malvolio might use a deep, authoritative tone when he delivers this line ✓. He often feels superior to those around him and this would show that he feels he has higher status than Cesario ✓. Malvolio might deliver the first part of his speech using a fast pace ✓ showing that he doesn't really want to spend any longer than he has to conversing with Cesario and is annoyed at having the spend his time chasing after him ✓.

When Cesario says he doesn't want the ring, Malvolio might become harsher in his tone, he might lower his voice and almost hiss ✓ the line

```
(line 12) MALVOLIO: Come, sir, you peevishly threw it to her; and her
                   will is, it should be so returned.
```

showing that he does not like Cesario's audacity in refusing him ✓. He might use a sneering tone when he says '*sir*' and emphasise '*peevishly*' ✓ to show his distaste at what he sees as Cesario's bad manners ✓.

The second question

The 6 mark question also casts you as a performer, and might look like this:

> **8(a)(ii) You are going to play Viola. As a performer, give three suggestions of how you would use performance skills to play this role from the start of the extract to the end. (6 marks)**

You will receive one mark (✓) for each suggestion and one mark (✓) for each appropriate reason. Think about:

- Movement, gesture
- Body language, posture
- Facial expressions including eye contact
- Vocal skills

COMPONENT 3: THEATRE MAKERS IN PRACTICE

When Viola moves as Cesario she is pretending to be male so you might consider a stiff, upright posture with strong, square shoulders and chin raised up slightly ✓. This contrasts to when you are Viola, who is likely have a softer stance ✓ not only because she is female but because she has been working hard to pretend to be someone else ✓.

As Cesario you are being confronted by Malvolio so you might decide to not use the stage space much ✓ to try to show strength and that you are not intimidated by him ✓. However, when he exits you might slump your shoulders and begin to pace ✓ as you realise that Olivia has fallen in love with you and the situation is becoming complicated ✓.

Vocally, your voice might be deeper and slower as Cesario ✓, again because of the pretence of being a man but also because Malvolio is being rude to you and you want to exude strength ✓. As Viola, your voice might be higher and faster paced ✓ as you become yourself but start to worry about the difficulties you are now in ✓.

The third question

The third, fourth and fifth questions ask you to imagine you are a director and then a designer working on the play. In order to prepare for this part of the exam you must have made all the production decisions you would make if you were indeed directing or designing it: it is not enough just to have got to know the text and made character or acting decisions.

Research past productions and have in mind a set design. Choose a form of stage layout from those explained on pages 10-11 of this book. You also need to know where people might be on the stage at key moments, entrances and exits, the position and style of any furniture, costumes, and so on. All decisions must be ones you know how to justify.

Context is extremely important. Make sure as part of your revision that you thoroughly research the context of both the time and place in which the play was written, and the time and place in which it is set. Try the search term 'Elizabethan life'. The context will form the basis for some of your answers.

Here is an example of the third question:

> 8(b)(i) As a director, discuss how you would use one of the production elements below to bring this extract to life for your audience. You should make reference to the context in which the text was created and performed.
> (9 marks)
>
> Choose one of the following:
> - Costume
> - Staging
> - Props/stage furniture

If you choose costume:

You could refer to how you would use costume to set the play in the Elizabethan period. Men in Elizabethan times would have worn breeches (short trousers) with stockings underneath. On top they would have worn a doublet, a type of tight fitted jacket often with a ruff around the neck. Malvolio is Olivia's servant but he is the head servant so has some status, equally, Cesario (Viola) is a servant for Duke Orsino so they would be reasonably well dressed as they are representing important households. As the pair meet in the street it is likely that they would be wearing hats and cloaks. Malvolio is a dour, miserable character who might wear black to suit his gloomy character. Cesario might be wearing dark green or blue, both fairly common choices showing Viola's wish to remain hidden.

You might make the decision to bring the play up to date and use contemporary costumes. Malvolio might wear an expensive suit to demonstrate his status. However, Malvolio has a very high opinion of himself so he might have some accessories to demonstrate this, perhaps a very expensive watch or other piece of jewellery to indicate that he aspires for his status to be higher than it is.

If you choose **staging**:

Staging is another term for **blocking**; deliberate choices about where the performers stand and how they move on stage to communicate character relationships and plot, and to create interesting stage pictures in relation to the set, **props** and audience. You might opt for the traditional Elizabethan **thrust stage** or you could consider setting your production **in the round**. Setting it in the round would mean that the audience would be surrounding the action and this can change how they experience what is happening on stage. You will need to consider how Viola will use the stage space to include the whole audience.

Choosing to set your production in the round would also mean that the actors enter and exit through the audience. Malvolio throwing the ring to the floor and exiting irritably through the audience could have quite a dramatic effect.

If you choose **props/stage furniture**:

The twelfth night after Christmas (6 January) marks the end of the Christmas celebrations. In Elizabethan times this was the end of the winter festival and on this day celebrations not only involved food, but things being reversed and turned upside down: the status of servants and masters celebrating might be reversed for the evening, for example. This topsy-turvy world is reflected in the play. You could choose to set the stage with props/stage furniture that relate to the end of Christmas celebrations, whether you are choosing to set the play in a modern or traditional context.

The fourth question

This question also asks you to think from the perspective of a director:

> 8(b)(ii) Viola is disguised as Cesario for most of the play. This scene is one of the few times that she is able to be herself. As a director, discuss how the performer playing this role might demonstrate the characters of Viola and Cesario in this extract and the complete play. (12 marks)
>
> You must consider:
> - Voice
> - Physicality
> - Stage directions and stage space

COMPONENT 3: THEATRE MAKERS IN PRACTICE

In your response you must show an understanding of how a director works with a performer in a specific role within the given extract, but then you should also **link** this understanding to the whole text.

When Viola first answers Malvolio

> (line 2) VIOLA: Even now, sir; on a moderate pace I have since
> arrived but hither.

She is portraying the role of Cesario, so her voice would be low pitched ✓ to keep the pretence that she is a man ✓. She would also want to appear to have strength and might use a stern tone ✓ to indicate that she doesn't like the fact that he is questioning her ✓. Malvolio is Olivia's servant and so would deserve a certain level of respect ✓. Viola might show this physically by bowing slightly or using limited eye contact ✓. At this point in the scene Viola might be on the opposite side of the stage to Malvolio ✓ as she was on her way home when he approached her ✓.

When Malvolio *throws the ring on the ground* he is being disrespectful to Viola. Viola might take on a more indignant tone ✓ when she replies

> (line 11) VIOLA: She took the ring of me: I'll none of it.

Viola would be offended by Malvolio's actions because she is of noble birth herself, and as such would not be used to rudeness. Physically, she might make herself more masculine in her posture by standing upright with squared shoulders and a strong chin ✓ demonstrating her annoyance by holding eye contact with Malvolio ✓. She might move towards him, closing the distance between them ✓ in an effort to show strength ✓.

When Malvolio *exits*, Viola is alone and so no longer has to pretend to be Cesario. She could immediately change her posture by relaxing her face and shoulders and perhaps becoming more feminine by leading with her hip or putting a hand on her hip ✓. During this whole speech Olivia can be herself, so her tone of voice would become higher pitched and softer ✓. On the line

> (line 18) VIOLA:... She made good view of me

Viola might use a stereotypically feminine gesture such as twirling her hair ✓.

Viola's realises that Olivia has fallen in love with her. On the line

> (line 21) VIOLA:... She loves me sure; the cunning of her passion
> Invites me in this churlish messenger.

she might sigh heavily and used a distressed tone, she might put her hands to her head and show how bad she feels by using a furrowed brow and clenching her eyes shut in torment ✓.

Viola is distraught by the love triangle that she has found herself in. On the lines

> (line 32) VIOLA:... My master loves her dearly;
> And I, poor monster, fond as much on him;
> And she, mistaken, seems to dote on me.
> What will become of this?

she might pace rapidly and use her arms emphatically, or use an open hand gesture to show that she is confused and upset while trying to make sense of the situation she has accidentally found herself in ✓.

In contrast to this scene you could explore Act 5 scene 1, when Viola and Sebastian are reunited. At first Viola would be keeping up her masculine stance as Cesario. Consider the line, *Sebastian was my father; such a Sebastian was my brother too, so went he suited to his watery tomb'* (line 227-229) – but as the twins realise who the other is, Viola would slowly transform from Cesario into herself.

Her voice might become higher pitched with excitement ✓ as well as letting go of the disguise, her posture could being to relax starting with her shoulders and moving towards her hips as she takes on a more feminine stance ✓.

The pair might begin the scene quite far apart but as the truth begins to emerge, the space between them on stage could narrow as they move towards each other ✓. The audience already know who is who and by this time are ready for the truth to be revealed. By the time Viola says *'if nothing lets to make us happy both, but this my masculine usurped attire,'* (line 244-245) she might have transformed back into her female form ✓.

Stephen Fry (Malvolio) and Mark Rylance (Olivia) in the Globe Theatre production of *Twelfth Night*, 2012

COMPONENT 3: THEATRE MAKERS IN PRACTICE

The fifth question

You will notice that each question has carried more marks than the one before, so you must write a little more for each answer. A final 14 mark question might look like this:

> **8(c) There are specific choices in this extract for designers. Discuss how you would use one design element to enhance the production of this extract for the audience. (14 marks)**
>
> Choose one of the following:
> - Set
> - Lighting
> - Sound

In answering this question it is important that you show your ability to use appropriate technical language and justify how your choices would enhance the extract for the audience.

If you choose **set**, for example, you might consider use of levels. Malvolio could enter the stage on a higher level to Viola, perhaps a raised platform running in front of the shopfronts/houses on the street. Having Malvolio higher up will mean he is physically as well as metaphorically looking down on Viola as he confronts her. Perhaps you might use some steps so that he can come down as he approaches Viola or he might remain elevated throughout the whole exchange.

You could consider having a very naturalistic set with real doors to represent the street and props to show the time of year in which the play was originally performed e.g. shopfronts/houses with Christmas wreaths or a painted backdrop to create the right atmosphere. Perhaps the backdrop is just of a wall, adding to Viola's feelings of loneliness at this stage.

The play could be set in winter, and the scene takes place on a street, so you might use **lighting** to give a wintry feel, consider the use of blues, which would work well with Viola's feeling of anguish when Malvolio exits.

Other productions, such as the 1996 film directed by Trevor Nunn, have very successfully set the play in a Mediterranean summer environment, however – based on the supposed 'real' location of Illyria. This would alter your choice of colour and lighting effects.

Think about how you might use live or recorded **sound** to create atmosphere in this scene. You might consider the sound of people celebrating to contrast with Viola being alone on stage and her confusion and upset. The sounds of live musicians playing festive or other music would further add to this. Alternatively, you could consider the use of birdsong to enhance the illusion of an outside street scene.

> The stage layout and design pages of this book can help you in your decisions. Turn to pages 10-11 and 156-171. Researching previous productions is also an excellent source of inspiration.

DNA
by Dennis Kelly

The context of the play

Commissioned by the National Theatre in London as part of their *Connections* festival, and first performed in 2007, the plot of *DNA* revolves around a disaffected and alienated teenage gang in an unspecified present day setting.

The power struggles within the group and the volatility of certain characters create plenty of dramatic tension. The core themes of self and group identity, bullying, cruelty and responsibility make the play highly accessible and appealing for young people to engage with.

The vocabulary is all straightforward and current. As you explore the text though, look at how each character speaks, as the writer has been specific in the style and words given to each role. The way each one uses language indicates such things as their status and their intelligence which are important for the ways you would interpret the role and discuss it in the exam. Leah's speeches, for example, require close exploration as she is often not talking about the plot. Look closely at what Leah says as it gives a context for the behaviours of the gang as a whole. She refers to the world around her and how it may have influenced her and them all to behave as they have.

A plot summary

The play opens with Mark and Jan discussing the revelation that someone is *'dead'*.

The next scene moves to the assembled gang of teenagers discussing the same fact. When Mark and Jan arrive they explain their version of events leading up to the victim, Adam, falling from the grille over a deep, disused shaft, to his apparent death. It becomes clear that they dared Adam to walk on the grille and then threw stones at him. They are all guilty – either specifically here, or because of their past bullying of the victim. Phil finally speaks and devises an elaborate plan. He suggests they invent a story in which Adam was seen with a flasher in the woods. They decide to throw a jumper of Adam's into some nearby bushes after getting a random stranger's DNA on it: making a 'crime scene'.

Though we don't see it, the plan is acted out and soon the audience learns that the police have, using the DNA on Adam's located jumper, found a man that fits the description of the man that Phil concocted. Worse than this – the suspect was on the police system for previous unspecified offences.

Brian is made to go and lie to the police at an identity parade to further incriminate the innocent suspect.

Then Jan and Mark reveal that Cathy has *'found someone'* in the woods. It turns out to be Adam. After his fall, Adam has been living in a hedge. He has clearly sustained a head injury. Aware of the problems that a now alive Adam could cause, Phil shows Cathy how to kill Adam by tying a plastic bag around Brian's head. Leah begs him not to do this.

COMPONENT 3: THEATRE MAKERS IN PRACTICE

By the end of the play, they have all got away with what they have done to Adam, but each one is changed as a result.

Leah and Phil in *DNA* at the National Theatre, 2008

The characters

Writer Dennis Kelly specifies that *'Names and genders of characters are suggestions only and can be changed to suit performers'*. They do though have different personalities, traits and specific functions for the storyline:

MARK and JAN act as the 'chorus' or narrators. They fill in blanks for the audience. They may well be younger and appear unable to act without reassurance and instruction from others.

LEAH is sensible and able both to think for herself and speak her mind. She does though follow the leadership of Phil and seems desperate for his attention and approval.

PHIL is on stage in many scenes, but rarely speaks. Although quiet for a long time, Phil clearly considers everyone's words and actions before he speaks. He gives calm and considered instructions to each member of the group as he assigns roles and tasks for them to complete. He appears dangerous.

JOHN TATE only appears in one scene. He is the leader of the gang, using fear to control others. However, he is visibly falling apart when we first meet him, panicking and unable to work out what the gang will do following Adam's 'accident'.

CATHY is shown to have no remorse about the groups' actions, finding it exciting. By the end of the play we learn that Cathy is now in charge and appears to have a sadistic nature.

RICHARD initially seems to be a strong character and potentially someone who is able to be a leader of the group. He gets left behind though and in the end becomes a character for others to boss around.

BRIAN is the weakest. He is bullied and pushed around by the group who choose him to be the one to lie directly to the police. He cannot deal with his guilt and is prescribed medication to help him cope.

DANNY is presented as a sensible character who starts with a plan – to be a dentist – with clear goals and intentions to use school positively. Shocked by what the group descend into, he still doesn't tell on them.

LOU will follow whoever the leader is at the time. She is a 'yes' girl, controlled by fear.

ADAM is the victim. What we learn about him is what we get by the reporting of Jan and Mark. We never get to see the 'real' him because he appears only briefly, and with a head injury from his fall.

Sample questions

As well as the question paper, you will get a source booklet with the extracts from each of the set texts on offer. You will only have studied one text, so find the extract you need in the source booklet and don't worry about the rest. The extract will be roughly 3 pages long in the source booklet and will link to roughly 4 pages from the copy of the text you are recommended to use in class.

In the question paper, the first line will say:

'You are involved in staging a production of this play. Please read the extract on page X of the source booklet.'

Look over the extract, which should be familiar to you from your study in class and your revision. Then begin to respond to the questions. It is recommended that you spend an hour on this section of the exam.

Remember: you are responding as a performer, director or designer. This is not English literature – it's Drama.

The sample questions on the next few pages relate to the following extract from pages 23-26 of the prescribed Oberon edition of *DNA*. You will need to apply the suggestions made for the sample questions to the extract and questions you are given. If your preparation and understanding is good enough, it makes no difference whether you have practised the exact questions or not, you will be able to adapt.

```
JOHN TATE: Dead. He's dead.
    Cathy says you're clever.
    So. What do we do?
    Pause. They all stare at LEAH and PHIL.
    LEAH goes to say something, but nothing comes out.
    Silence.
    More silence.
    PHIL puts his Coke carefully on the ground.
PHIL: Cathy, Danny, Mark, you go to Adam's house, you wait until
    his mum's out, you break in.                                    5
DANNY: What?
PHIL: through an upstairs window so it's out of the way, make sure
```

no one sees you. Get in, go to his bedroom, find a pair of his
shoes and an item of his clothing, a jumper, or something,
don't touch the jumper, that's very important, do not touch
the jumper, but you have to get it in the plastic bag
without touching it.

CATHY: What plastic bag?

PHIL: The refuse sacks that you are going to buy on the way,
do not use the first one on the roll, use the third or fourth,
do not be tempted to use a bin liner you have knocking around
the house as that will be a DNA nightmare. Richard, you take
Brian to the Head, tell him that you found Brian crying in
the toilets, asked him what was wrong and when he told you,
you brought him here.

RICHARD: Me? But I hate him!

PHIL: Brian, you cry.

RICHARD: Me with Brian?

PHIL: and you tell them a man showed you his willy in the woods.

BRIAN: Wha…what?

PHIL: by the bridge, last week, a fat Caucasian male, 5'9" say,
with thinning hair and a postman's uniform, sad eyes, softly
spoken.

DANNY: Who's that?

PHIL: The man who showed Brian his willy in the woods, please
keep up, I'm making this up as I go along.

DANNY: What were his teeth like?

PHIL: Bad, very bad.

DANNY: Thought so.

PHIL: Lou, Danny and Jan you take the shoes, Lou you put them on,
and you enter the woods from the south entrance.

CATHY: Which one's south?

MARK: By the Asda.

PHIL: Danny you enter from the east entrance with Jan on your back.

DANNY: Is he taking the piss?

PHIL: The weight of the two of you combined should equal that of
a fat postman with bad teeth, you make your way into the woods,
do not put her down unless it's on concrete or a tree trunk,
never when you're walking on mud. You meet Lou near the bridge,
you move around a bit, you exit from the south.

MARK: By the Asda.

PHIL: Cathy and Mark you meet them there, but on the way you find
a quiet street, you wait until it's just you and a man, you
walk ahead of him and when you're far ahead you drop the jumper.
The man picks it up, runs after you covering it in DNA and then

> gives it back, make sure you let him drop it in the bag,
> say you're taking it to a charity shop. Take it to the south
> entrance, tear it a little, chuck it in a hedge, all go home
> and wait a day or two until Adam's declared missing and then
> John Tate comes forward and says he thinks he saw Adam with a   55
> fat man in a uniform by Asda but he can't be sure, they'll think
> he's been abducted, they'll be enquiries, police, mourning, a
> service and if everyone keeps their mouth shut we should be fine.
> Any questions?
> *They stare at him open mouthed.*
> *He bends down. Picks up his Coke.*
> *Starts to drink his Coke.*

The first question

The first question requires you to imagine you are a performer in the play. A possible question might be:

> **5(a) There are specific choices in this extract for performers.**
>
> (i) You are going to play Danny. Explain two ways you would use vocal skills to play this character in this extract. (4 marks)

For your response you will get one mark (✓) for each way identified and an additional mark (✓) for each linked explanation. For example, you might refer to:

- Pitch and tone of delivery
- Pace and volume of delivery
- Use of pause.

In discussing the use of voice you must demonstrate your understanding of the character as well. Here are some ideas, but you wouldn't need them all – it's only a 4 mark question.

For example:

> (line 6) DANNY: What?

In saying this line as a performer playing Danny you might have a louder volume ✓ to indicate your shock at the strange sounding plan that Phil is beginning to outline ✓.

Another example from the extract could be:

> (line 40) DANNY: Is he taking the piss?

In saying this line as a performer playing Danny you may speed up the pace of the delivery ✓ because the line is said in instant disbelief as Phil is suggesting you carry Jan into the woods on your back and you fail to see how this is part of a serious plan ✓. Alternatively, you might suggest that there is a high pitch ✓ in the delivery to indicate the surprise at Phil's suggestion and that you think you are being made to look stupid ✓.

COMPONENT 3: THEATRE MAKERS IN PRACTICE

The second question

The 6 mark question also casts you as a performer, and might look like this:

> **5(a)(ii) You are going to play Phil. He rises in his authority in this extract, taking charge of the plan for the group to cover up what has happened. (6 marks)**
>
> As a performer, give three suggestions of how you would use performance skills to show his authority in this extract. You must provide a reason for each suggestion.

In your response you will get one mark (✓) for each suggestion and one mark (✓) for each appropriate reason. For example:

- Use of space
- Body language
- Facial gesture
- Posture
- Eye contact
- Vocal delivery – tone, pitch, pace, pause, volume
- Gesture.

You could again refer to vocal delivery, for example:

> (line 59) PHIL: Any questions?

You could outline how you intend to say this in an assured tone with an even pace ✓ to demonstrate how confident you are that what you have just come up with as a plan is what everyone should and will now follow ✓.

You might also refer to body language and eye contact, for example on the stage direction:

> He bends down. Picks up his Coke. Starts to drink his Coke.

You could refer to the casual, calm body language ✓ he adopts in picking up the can as if carefree and confident ✓. You might also say that he will not be making eye contact ✓ on this stage direction, showing that he isn't seeking their approval for the plan, demonstrating his status and assured nature ✓.

You might refer to gesture, such as on the line:

> (line 33) PHIL: Bad, very bad.

Here you are responding to a question from Danny about what the fake suspect's teeth were like. Going with his odd question – which you know is part of his fixation with dentistry as a potential career – you might respond with a slight smile ✓ showing that you are building confidence in the lie and the fake suspect you are creating ✓. Alternatively the smile could indicate a willingness to play along with Danny's absurd question because you are happy for a moment of light relief and you realise the question means Danny is starting to agree and show that he will go along with your plan ✓.

The third question

The third, fourth and fifth questions ask you to imagine you are a director and then a designer working on the play. In order to prepare for this part of the exam you must have made all the production decisions you would make if you were indeed directing or designing it: it is not enough just to have got to know the text and made character or acting decisions.

Research past productions and have in mind a set design. Choose a form of stage layout from those explained on pages 10-11 of this book. You also need to know where people might be on the stage at key moments, entrances and exits, the position and style of any furniture, costumes, and so on. All decisions must be ones you know how to justify.

Context is extremely important. Make sure as part of your revision that you thoroughly research the context of both the time and place in which the play was written, and the time and place in which it is set. In this case, both might be the present day. The context will form the basis for some of your answers.

Here is an example of the third question:

> 5(b)(i) As a director, discuss how you would use one of the production elements below to bring this extract to life for your audience. You should make reference to the context in which the text was created and performed. (9 marks)
>
> Choose one of the following:
> - costume
> - staging
> - props/stage furniture

In your response, if choosing costume, you could refer to:

How you would use costume to indicate the contemporary time period of the piece and/or the status of the characters. As the group of teenagers are in fact a tightly knit gang ✓ you might use costume to unite them ✓. They may have similar styled outfits to visually connect them, such as casual sports gear ✓. You may decide that they each have their own style, but they have a signature piece of clothing that unites them, such as a hoodie ✓ which would also link to an outfit associated stereotypically with gang violence. Maybe they have a scruffy school uniform ✓ to remind us of their age, but worn in such a way as we can tell they don't follow the rules ✓. As demonstrated, in each case you must justify your ideas. Pages 156–159 of this book could help you with your choices.

Costumes in the National Theatre's 2008 production of *DNA*

COMPONENT 3: THEATRE MAKERS IN PRACTICE

In your response if choosing staging you could refer to:

Entrances and exits. Type of staging. Sight lines. Levels. Staging is another term for **blocking**; deliberate choices about where the performers stand and how they move on stage to communicate character relationships and plot, and to create interesting stage pictures in relation to the set, **props** and audience. In each case you must justify your ideas just as for the costume example.

In your response, if choosing props/stage furniture you could refer to:

Props within the space and/or personal props (as appropriate) to help indicate character, time period and location or symbolic meaning. In each case again you must justify your ideas, just as was shown in the costume example.

In all answers the audience should be central to the response. You could be symbolic in your choices; you don't have to go with naturalism.

The fourth question

This question also asks you to think from the perspective of a director:

> **5(b)(ii)** Brian is picked on by the group who force him to act out the hardest parts of their plan in order to get away with what has happened to Adam.
> As a director, discuss how the performer playing this role might demonstrate his status and his frail state of mind to the audience in this extract and the complete play. (12 marks)
>
> You must consider:
> - voice
> - physicality
> - stage directions and stage space

In your response you must show an understanding of how a director works with a performer in a specific role within the given extract, but then you should also **link** this understanding to the whole text.

In this extract Brian only has one line, but he's on stage the whole time and is a crucial part of Phil's plan. Though often silent, there is much you could discuss for his role here and then with reference to the play as a whole.

> (line 25) Brian: Wha...what?

You could discuss how Brian's line shows how shocked he is that Phil suggests he should lie to the Head and say a man flashed him in the woods ✓. To show the shock, this line could be delivered with a higher pitch ✓ and with a wide-eyed facial expression ✓. For the rest of the scene, to show how anxious he is getting with the whole plan ✓ he might curl up and not make eye contact ✓. In later scenes, this could be a repeated sign of him trying to comfort himself, but to show a worsening state of mind he might also rock himself ✓.

For example, when the group are telling Brian that he will have to identify a suspect the police have found (page 39) he is crying and here an increase in the rocking action and a continued lack of eye contact would be appropriate ✓. At this moment, shaking his head ✓ and mumbling underneath what they say to him ✓ could also be successful at showing how their bullying is making him feel increased anxiety ✓. Later, when Adam is found, unexpectedly alive, Brian appears to have suffered a complete mental breakdown. He talks about feeling like the trees are watching him and that he's always wanted to rub his face in the earth (page 50). In highlighting the breakdown, maybe this presents an opportunity to play Brian in a contrasting way to previous scenes ✓. He could be played here with an excited tone ✓ with loud volume ✓ and with expansive, unrestrained movements ✓. He could be far less 'curled up' at this point, and, guided by the stage directions, he could be freely moving around the space/environment, like a child out of control ✓.

These suggestions are only a starting point, remember that you're looking to achieve 12 marks for this question and be sure to write enough.

The fifth question

You will notice that each question has carried more marks than the one before, so you must write a little more for each answer. A final 14 mark question might look like this:

> 5(c) There are specific choices in this extract for designers. Discuss how you would use one design element to enhance the production of this extract for the audience. (14 marks)
>
> Choose one of the following:
> - Set
> - Lighting
> - Sound

If you choose **set** as your design element, for example, this scene takes place in the woods, therefore you could use projections of trees ✓. But you could also choose not to go for naturalism, and be symbolic instead. You could also perhaps discuss having levels created by stage blocks ✓ which indicate status ✓.

The woodland setting should also give you lots of ideas for **lighting** and **sound**. For example, you could have a gobo projecting speckles on the floor to represent sunlight through trees ✓, and also perhaps a green tinged wash through this light to add to the effect of the setting in the woods ✓. You could go for symbolic lighting, i.e. a red wash to indicate the scene's tension ✓ and maybe a spotlight picking out Phil ✓ growing brighter ✓ to show a rise in his status as he takes his role as leader of the group ✓.

For sounds, you could go naturalistic, i.e. the sound of wind gently rustling the leaves ✓, or you could underscore with music to build the tension ✓.

> The stage layout and design pages of this book can help you in your decisions. Turn to pages 10-11 and 156-171. Researching previous productions is also an excellent source of inspiration.

COMPONENT 3: THEATRE MAKERS IN PRACTICE

1984
by George Orwell, Robert Icke and Duncan Macmillan

The context of the play

Big Brother and Room 101 might be known to you now as TV programmes, but they were originally ideas which formed part of George Orwell's novel, Nineteen Eighty-Four.

First published in 1948, Orwell turned the 48 round to make 84, thinking it might take until then for the world he described to become a reality. It's a world created by mankind, a hell on earth of extreme political correctness, torture and terror.

Some argue that the totalitarian society Orwell imagined has been seen in Nazi Germany, the former Soviet Union and other dictatorships and regimes. 'If you want a picture of the future, Winston, imagine a boot stamping on a human face – for ever.' Labelled 'political satire' in this exam, this play is an interpretation which uses many of the key plot points from the original novel and turns them into a compelling stage story.

In many ways it's a warning against totalitarianism, and many people in politics have claimed it supports their own views about the danger from others. However, it's very much open to a personal response and makes for a challenging, thought-provoking experience when performed.

The authors' notes on pages 8-10 of the prescribed text are very useful in explaining about the original novel and its controversial mock-historical Appendix which inspired some of the play and sheds new light on Orwell's intentions. The best background to this play is to read George Orwell's original novel, but there is also a film version starring John Hurt.

A plot summary

The central character, Winston Smith, thinks a thought, starts a diary and falls in love. These are all forbidden, criminal actions and the ever-watchful eyes of Big Brother are on him.

He's persuaded to let his natural rebellious feelings out, to shout hatred of Big Brother and to read a book supposedly written by the state's arch enemy.

His secrets are discovered and he's tortured by the enigmatic O'Brien who may or may not be a rebel. Smith is put in Room 101, where people being tortured find 'the worst thing in the world,' the thing the victim dreads the most. In Smith's case it's rats. His sheer terror forces him to betray his lover Julia and the play ends with him 'cured', loving and thanking Big Brother.

The play uses technology to show how history can be rewritten and people made as if they never existed. The short, sharp scenes, multi-roling of minor characters and atmosphere of tense, dangerous activities crushed by an invincible source makes it a very accessible theatrical experience.

Original production of this adaptation of *1984*, Playhouse Theatre, 2014

The characters

WINSTON SMITH the protagonist, late 30s, thin; the rebel.

O'BRIEN wears spectacles and smart clothes; powerful, with a voice like a doctor, teacher or priest, representing both authority and rebellion; a kind of Big Uncle to Smith.

CHARRINGTON keeper of the antiques shop who tempts Smith to buy a diary and use his back room for his love sessions; not as safe as he seems.

MARTIN a character who mouths official instructions; he narrates some of the action and is described by O'Brien as 'one of us.'

SYME a work colleague of Smith, gives information about the 'benefits' of Newspeak; dislikes Parsons. He is 'unpersoned' before the end of the play.

PARSONS a work colleague and neighbour of Smith, wears shorts in canteen, is proud of his daughter for denouncing criminals, even when she denounces him!

MRS PARSONS agrees with her husband; she is described as 'a metre wide.'

JULIA a waitress who becomes Smith's lover; a rebel, tempting him to crimes. She says she hates purity and wants the Party 'to rot from the inside.'

VOICE becomes **HOST** – described as man in his 60s, 'a gentle, benevolent presence.' He also plays Charrington.

COMPONENT 3: THEATRE MAKERS IN PRACTICE

MAN a man in a crowd who expresses official views through his comments; he also plays Syme.

MOTHER – Winston's mother in the flashback also plays Mrs Parsons

FATHER also plays Mr Parsons.

PARSONS' CHILD is a smart 7-year old girl, finds and uses a remote control; denounces Winston Smith and also plays Winston's sister in the flashback.

WOMAN'S VOICE is an exercise commander.

the **TELESCREEN** is the voice of Big Brother.

SPEAKWRITE is the automated voice of a machine that deletes people's history.

a **THOUGHTCRIMINAL** confesses his 'crimes' on screen.

Page to stage

The **actor's skills** include the bringing of characters to life, believably and credibly in often short scenes and working with the stage effects required by the authors. There's little time during the play for characters to develop deep roles, full of empathy or tragedy. This is a form of narrative drama.

The **director's role** is to bring the separate actors' character interpretations together to make the play accessible to an audience. It's also to make stage effects work and the narrative unfold in a way that involves the audience, who must deal with some shocking, unpleasant scenes.

The **designer's role** is to work with both director and actors to ensure each scene captures place – an unspecified room which becomes a corridor and Smith's room, the canteen, the torture area and Room 101, and to create the special effects so that the audience is assisted in its journey through the performance.

Sample questions

As well as the question paper, you will get a source booklet with the extracts from each of the set texts on offer. You will only have studied one text, so find the extract you need in the source booklet and don't worry about the rest. The extract will be roughly 3 pages long in the source booklet and will link to roughly 4 pages from the copy of the text you are recommended to use in class.

In the question paper, the first line will say:

'You are involved in staging a production of this play. Please read the extract on page X of the source booklet.'

Look over the extract, which should be familiar to you from your study in class and your revision. Then begin to respond to the questions. It is recommended that you spend an hour on this section of the exam.

Remember: you are responding as a performer, director or designer. This is not English literature – it's Drama.

The sample questions on the next few pages relate to the following extract from pages 86-88 of the prescribed Oberon edition of *1984*. You will need to apply the suggestions made for the sample questions to the extract and questions you are given. If your preparation and understanding is good enough, it makes no difference whether you have practised the exact questions or not, you will be able to adapt.

O'BRIEN: When I told you that you could ask me anything, there was one question that immediately came to mind. You were afraid to ask it because you already knew the answer.

The worst thing in the world varies from individual to individual. It may be burial alive, or death by fire, or by drowning, or by impalement.

Ask the question Winston.

WINSTON: Where am I now?

O'BRIEN: Where do you think you are?

WINSTON: I think …
I think this is Room 101.

O'BRIEN: And what's in Room 101?

WINSTON: The thing that's in Room 101 is the worst thing in the world.

An ANIMAL HANDLER wheels a trolley onto the stage with great care, accompanied by some TORTURERS. They wear thick gloves and protective masks. On the trolley is a large metal box.

O'BRIEN: In your case, Winston, the worst thing in the world happens to be rats.

WINSTON: No.

O'BRIEN: You understand this construction. The mask will fit over your head, leaving no exit. The rats will begin in the front section of the cage, with two gates between them and your face. Once the mask is installed the first gate will open and the rats, desperate to escape, will come closer. You will be able to smell them. You can bring things to a close whenever you choose. You know that. Nothing is happening that you did not foresee.

WINSTON: No. I can't. I can't.

O'BRIEN: The rats are starving. Once the second gate is opened, they will leap onto your face and bore straight into it. Sometimes they attack the eyes first. Sometimes the tongue.

We hear the rats - squealing, tearing, scratching.

WINSTON: Please. You can't.

O'BRIEN: It is an instinct which cannot be disobeyed. It is the same with you. They are a form of pressure that you cannot withstand, even if

you wished to. You know what you need to
do.

WINSTON: I don't! What is it? What is it? How can I
do it if I don't know what —

O'BRIEN: Now, Winston, you know that already. You 45
have always known it.

The word 'Julia' appears.
The TORTURORS raise the contraption and prepare to attach it to WINSTON'S face. WINSTON moans in terror.

When hungry or agitated, rats can strip all
the flesh from a human face in a matter of minutes.

They show astonishing intelligence in
knowing when someone is helpless. 50

Winston looks at people in the audience and pleads with them.

WINSTON: HOW CAN YOU JUST SIT THERE?
GET UP! DO SOMETHING! HELP ME
— HELP ME — YOU HAVE TO STOP
THEM — PLEASE GET UP — PLEASE —
I'M SORRY — NO — I'M SORRY 55

The mask is attached to WINSTON'S face.

O'BRIEN: I am going to open the first gate.

WINSTON: STOP IT! PLEASE STOP — I CAN'T —

O'Brien opens the first gate.

O'BRIEN: I AM YOUR FRIEND Winston. I'm trying to
Help you.
I am now going to open the second gate. 60

O'BRIEN prepares to open the gate.

WINSTON: JULIA! JULIA!
DO IT TO JULIA! DO IT TO JULIA!
I DON'T CARE WHAT YOU DO TO
HER. TEAR HER FACE OFF, RIP HER
FLESH TO PIECES JUST DO IT TO 65
HER! NOT ME! JULIA! JULIA! DO IT
TO JULIA!

The lights black out. The sound of the rats is overwhelming.

GCSE DRAMA STUDY GUIDE

The first question

The first question requires you to imagine you are a performer in the play. A possible question might be:

> **1(a) There are specific choices in this extract for performers.**
>
> (i) You are going to play a torturer. He or she doesn't speak, but explain two ways you would use physical skills to play this character in this extract. You must provide a reason for each suggestion. (4 marks)

For your response you will get one mark (✓) for each way identified and an additional mark (✓) for each linked explanation. Here are some ideas, but you wouldn't need them all – it's only a 4 mark question. To answer this you could focus on some of the following:

Your mode of walking – the torturer enters accompanying an animal handler who is wheeling a trolley and a large metal box containing rats. You should think about how your physicality might show your feelings about this: Would you express your feelings in your movement or be more 'robotic' so as to remain anonymous and 'safe' in a dangerous environment? ✓

Your facial expressions – you could be smiling, admiring the rats as they are 'squealing, tearing, scratching' ✓, or perhaps you too are nervous of them and would show this in your face ✓. Winston becomes more uncomfortable as the scene progresses: as the torturer you could choose either to enjoy this ✓ or remain impassive ✓, each showing different sides to the character and taking into account the context of the story – in which no one is really safe.

Work with props: as the scene goes on, someone is required to raise the contraption and prepare to attach it, then fit the contraption on Winston's face. While you perform these actions you must maintain your role: are you clearly enjoying it? ✓ do you remain deadpan ✓ or even look concerned? ✓ Why? And how does your expression alter as Winston reaches the climax of his terror? ✓

The second question

The 6 mark question also casts you as a performer, and might look like this:

> **1(a)(ii)** You are going to play Winston. He is reduced to total terror and begs the audience – ' How can you just sit there? Get up, do something, help me!' As a performer, give three suggestions of how you would use performance skills to show you have been reduced to this pitiful begging. You must provide a reason for each suggestion. (6 marks)

To answer this you could focus on some of the following:

Use of **space**: your fear would increase as the rats are wheeled in ✓, if you are free to move about, perhaps you would become agitated and begin looking for an exit ✓ to demonstrate that having already had pain inflicted by electric shock, having his fingertips cut off and teeth pulled out when he was strapped down, now Winston would like to escape ✓.

Use of **physicality**: if Winston is still strapped down, perhaps you might struggle against the clips that hold you throughout ✓, even causing yourself more damage, to indicate your helplessness ✓.

Use of **voice**: broken, beaten, hurt and lost, when you ask

    (line 11) WINSTON: Where am I now?

it could be in a quiet voice ✓ to show that he is broken ✓. Winston hesitates ✓ when O'Brien asks him to say aloud his biggest fear, that this is Room 101, which demonstrate that he is so afraid he will be right, that he can't bring himself to say it ✓. When the rat mask is about to go on his head, his speech is written in capital letters indicating high volume ✓, you could begin shrieking at the audience for help to indicate that he is at the height of desperation ✓. The final cry ✓ as the second rat gate is about to open, is his betrayal of Julia, and you could make it at the top of your voice to show how desperate you are ✓.

The third question

The third, fourth and fifth questions ask you to imagine you are a director and then a designer working on the play. In order to prepare for this part of the exam you must have made all the production decisions you would make if you were indeed directing or designing it: it is not enough just to have got to know the text and made character or acting decisions.

Research past productions and have in mind a set design. Choose a form of stage layout from those explained on pages 10-11 of this book. You also need to know where people might be in the room at key moments, entrances and exits, the position and style of any furniture, costumes, and so on. All decisions must be ones you know how to justify.

Context is extremely important. Make sure as part of your revision that you thoroughly research the context of both the time and place in which the play was written, and the time and place in which it is set. Try researching the Soviet Union. The context will form the basis for some of your answers.

Here is an example of the third question:

1(b)(i) As a director, discuss how you would use one of the production elements below to bring this extract to life for your audience. You should make reference to the context in which the text was created and performed. (9 marks)

Choose one of the following:
- costume
- staging
- props/stage furniture

In your response, if choosing costume, you could describe how:

The standard uniform of all citizens in Oceania might be a functional work-set, like a factory worker might wear ✓, with O'Brien possibly in a different shade to indicate his status ✓. Torturers could be in a different shade again ✓ or white coats ✓. Maintain an awareness that the audience should understand the hierarchy ✓. However, because of the context you might decide that no other individualism is allowed ✓, that it should be timeless, uniform, practical and unflattering ✓.

Winston and Julia in the 2014 production

In your response if choosing staging you could refer to:

The importance of having an awareness of the audience in positioning the torture table or chair in the centre ✓, with or without a view of the door ✓ to add terror for Winston, and allowing wheeling in of the trolley ✓. Staging is another term for **blocking**; deliberate choices about where the performers stand and how they move on stage to communicate character relationships and plot, and to create interesting stage pictures in relation to the set, **props** and audience.

In your response, if choosing props/stage furniture you could refer to:

The chair or table with restraints ✓, the trolley carrying the metal box ✓, and the mask apparatus to attach to Winston's face should all be gruesomely realistic ✓, even if only symbolic ✓ to make the audience both horrified and sympathetic to Winston at his barbaric treatment ✓. Any other furniture, you might decide, is functional, not attractive ✓.

Remember, the question asks you to refer to the context in which the text was created and performed – post-war Britain imagining a future tyranny where individualism is illegal and is punished. It's legitimate to stage this in and/or about other places where historically or currently despots have terrorised their own people.

COMPONENT 3: THEATRE MAKERS IN PRACTICE

The fourth question

This question also asks you to think from the perspective of a director:

> **1(b)(ii)** O'Brien is the character with the highest status throughout the play; he is next to Big Brother. As a director, discuss how the performer playing this role might demonstrate high status to the audience in this extract and the complete play. **(12 marks)**
>
> You must consider:
> - voice
> - physicality
> - stage directions and stage space

In your response you must show an understanding of how a director works with a performer in a specific role within the given extract, but then you should also **link** this understanding to the whole text.

To answer this you should focus on how director and actor work together to interpret the role which requires status and an authority that comes from his stature and physicality as well as his ability to destroy people.

You need to give reasons to support specific examples you choose. If you talk about what the director intends the audience to feel at a particular moment, what is the evidence and your understanding of **proxemics**, dialogue, **direct address**, and characters' thoughts in the play? What is the actor's and director's intention?

Voice – you could discuss how O'Brien speaks, almost always quietly, calmly, reasonably, as if he is sorry that Winston has to be tortured, giving examples. He is the voice of authority – he is normally obeyed. Often he is heard but not seen, his voice relayed to the stage. He enjoys debating with Winston and there is a slight sense of amusement that he can always outwit his victim.

Physicality – his physical presence must be commanding of both respect and fear. The way he stands, gestures, smiles, nods and walks at specific times must convey the power and authority he has and never releases, again with specific examples. He is in absolute control of everybody he deals with. While he is apparently betraying Big Brother (pages 57–61) he remains fully in command.

Stage space – with the punishment area central to the extract scene, there is scope for O'Brien to move around Winston, often coming close to talk to his face. He stands to the side while the rats are brought close. There must be some understanding of proxemics in use as their relationship develops through the play, and here as his interrogation turns to successful confession from Winston. Wherever he is placed in corridor or in a room, O'Brien demonstrates his power.

The fifth question

You will notice that each question has carried more marks than the one before, so you must write a little more for each answer. A final 14 mark question might look like this:

> 1(c) There are specific choices in this extract for designers.
>
> Discuss how you would use one design element to enhance the production of this extract for the audience. (14 marks)
>
> Choose one of the following:
>
> - Set
> - Lighting
> - Special effects

To answer this kind of question, you have to show *how* the element you choose from the list would enhance enjoyment and understanding for the audience in production of the extract on stage. What do you understand about production decisions the designer must make working with the director to move this text from page to stage?

If you choose **set** as your design element, for example, you should demonstrate how the design and positioning of the torture chair ✓ adds to the atmosphere, drawing the audience's attention in to the rats in the cage ✓, and enhances the portrayal of characters and how the audience is assisted in understanding the mood of the play. Is the O'Brien observation corridor used in this extract? ✓. Are there levels? ✓ What are the reasons for design decisions made?

If you choose **lighting**, there is a need to have some quite gloomy lighting throughout ✓; Oceania is at war ✓, there is little room for fun. A spotlight on the torture chair ✓ would highlight the action; perhaps a change in the lighting state ✓ when Winston realises he is in Room 101 ✓, and again when the '*sound of rats is overwhelming*' ✓. What are the reasons for your lighting decisions?

This play gives lots of scope for **special effects** – the rats may have to be symbolic ✓, but as the extract ends, the noise of their '*squealing, tearing, scratching*' has to rise to a climax ✓ to accompany Winston's breakdown and betrayal of Julia. What technology could be employed to make this effective for an audience? Could a projection of a close up of his face as the rats approach be helpful? ✓ What are the reasons for each special effects decision?

> **The stage layout and design pages of this book can help you in your decisions. Turn to pages 10-11 and 156-171. Researching previous productions is also an excellent source of inspiration**

COMPONENT 3: THEATRE MAKERS IN PRACTICE

Blue Stockings
by Jessica Swale

The context of the play

In the 19th century, girls were not expected to be educated beyond needlecraft, art, domestic sciences and possibly French. Wealthy girls often had governesses to teach them at home. University was not generally for women.

During the later part of the century Britain's first residential college for women was opened in Hitchin, later moving to Girton near Cambridge, where women's right to study for and be awarded a degree, equal with men, was fought for. It was significant that they were near the heart of male academic excellence in Cambridge.

'Blue stockings' was a phrase used to describe educated, intelligent, noble women in the 1800s who were regarded as 'unnatural.' The description was not flattering, certainly not at the time in which this play is set.

The play was first performed in a professional production at Shakespeare's Globe, London, in August 2013. Regardless of gender, age, or cultural background, the fight for equality appeals to and has something to say to today's audiences. There are some moments of humour and the passions of clashing beliefs make for good conflict drama.

A plot summary

Set in 1896, over twenty years before women secured the Parliamentary vote, the head of Girton College is determined that girls who study hard and equal men in every grade should graduate and not be regarded as unqualified and unmarriageable. Their studies should not become a stigma.

However, she and the women are up against entrenched views of senior male staff and most of the male students, who say things that would nowadays be regarded as sexist and patronising, but were of their time and widely shared, even by some women themselves.

To change things, a vote must be taken in the university to consider giving women the right to graduate – but only already qualified men may vote. The play follows four girls' struggles against male prejudice and bullying over a year. They fail, but pave the way for future successful changing of attitudes which as the play explains in the final back projection, didn't happen till 1948.

Blue Stockings in its original production at the Globe Theatre, 2013

The characters

TESS MOFFAT, described as a 'curious girl', is the main rebel, a natural leader, she nonetheless is capable of falling in love like anybody else.

CELIA WILLBOND, 'a fragile hard worker', is never distracted in her aims.

CAROLYN ADDISON is an early 'bohemian', who lives an unconventional life

MAEVE SULLIVAN is a 'mystery' female student who is capable of extremely principled action.

RALPH MAYHEW is a male student

LLOYD is a male student

HOLMES is a male student

EDWARDS is a male student

WILL BENNETT is a male student, Tess' friend from home

ELIZABETH WELSH is the Mistress of Girton College

DR HENRY MAUDSLEY is a psychiatrist after whom the Maudsley Hospital is named

MR BANKS, a lecturer at both Trinity and Girton, faces a dilemma regarding promotion if he gives up on teaching the women

COMPONENT 3: THEATRE MAKERS IN PRACTICE

MISS BLAKE, Girton lecturer, challenges students' thinking, makes intellectual jokes

PROFESSOR COLLINS

PROFESSOR ANDERSON

PROFESSOR RADLEIGH

MINNIE, a housemaid

MR PECK, a gardener/maintenance man

MISS BOTT, a loud knitter, chaperone to the young women

BILLY SULLIVAN, Maeve's brother

MRS LINDLAY, a shopkeeper

OTHERS: Librarian and more male students; lady and husband in the café.

A note in the playscript explains that apart from Elizabeth Welsh and Tess, all parts can be doubled, meaning it needs 12 actors to play it in full.

Page to stage

The **actor's skills** include the bringing of characters to life believably in often short scenes with little to say. Body language, voice, costume and set help actors perform, along with props, such as Tess riding a bicycle on stage in scene one.

The **director's role** is to bring the separate actors' interpretations of their characters into a line that makes the play accessible to an audience. The sympathy of today's audience is likely to lie with the Girton women and their supporters rather than most of the men.

The **designer's role** is to work with both director and actors to make each scene visually appropriate, to capture the place – outside, the teashop, the haberdashery and the classrooms so the actors are at home and the audience is assisted in its journey through the performance.

Sample questions

As well as the question paper, you will get a source booklet with the extracts from each of the set texts on offer. You will only have studied one text, so find the extract you need in the source booklet and don't worry about the rest. The extract will be roughly 3 pages long in the source booklet and will link to roughly 4 pages from the copy of the text you are recommended to use in class.

In the question paper, the first line will say:

'You are involved in staging a production of this play. Please read the extract on page X of the source booklet.'

Look over the extract, which should be familiar to you from your study in class and your revision. Then begin to respond to the questions. It is recommended that you spend an hour on this section of the exam.

Remember: you are responding as a performer, director or designer. This is not English literature – it's Drama.

The sample questions on the next few pages relate to the following extract from pages 86-88 of the prescribed Nick Hern edition of *Blue Stockings*. You will need to apply the suggestions made for the sample questions to the extract and questions you are given. If your preparation and understanding is good enough, it makes no difference whether you have practised the exact questions or not, you will be able to adapt.

DR MAUDSLEY: Let's abandon the fanciful speculation of the
    Europeans and instead turn our attention to more progressive
    theories. Anyone?

   TESS raises her hand. She is ignored.

   Come on, gentlemen? No one?

   *TESS continues to wait with her hand raised. LLOYD
   stands.*

LLOYD: Sir.

MAUDSLEY: Go ahead.

LLOYD: In your thesis, you write that hysteria is brought on by
    a weakened morality, mind or will. That any woman is
    susceptible.

MAUDSLEY: I do indeed. And that it leads to maladies
    such as –

LLOYD: Mania.

DR MAUDSLEY: Yes.

HOLMES: Lunacy.

DR MAUDSLEY: Yes.

EDWARDS: Paroxysm.

DR MAUDSLEY: Yes.

LLOYD: 'Feminism.'

   The MEN might laugh. TESS stands.

TESS: But, sir, I believe Charcot says hysteria is caused by
    specific biological weaknesses, not by a woman's lack of
    moral judgement at all. That it's hereditary.

   A ripple of consternation.

DR MAUDSLEY: Indeed he does. Did I invite you to stand,
    miss?

TESS: Moffat, sir.

DR MAUDSLEY: I wasn't asking your name. I'm not interested
    in your name. Are you contradicting me in my own lecture?

TESS: No –

DR MAUDSLEY: Are you suggesting these Europeans are
    superior to my colleagues and I? Are you an expert?

TESS: No, / sir –

DR MAUDSLEY: Have you undertaken experiments? In your
    own laboratory?

TESS: Of course not, but, sir, these scientists –

DR MAUDSLEY: They are not scientists, they are fantasists.
    Miss, why are you here? This is a lecture hall, not a laundry.

TESS: Sir!

DR MAUDSLEY: Gentlemen, it has been proven time and

COMPONENT 3: THEATRE MAKERS IN PRACTICE

again that hysteria results from a state of emotional agitation commonly observed in the female –

TESS: But there is no evidence to prove that / women alone are susceptible to hysteria, it's merely an observation –

DR MAUDSLEY: (*indicating* TESS) A woman becomes agitated as she relinquishes control of her emotions.

TESS: I am not agitated because I am a woman! / I am agitated Because you won't consider an alternative scientifically proven phenomenon. What about Freud?

DR MAUDSLEY: The temperature rises, nerves destabilise, the woman begins to hyperventilate. A perfect example of hysterical agitation, gentlemen, leading to mania.

TESS: Why won't you acknowledge other people's theories?

DR MAUDSLEY: I do. Why can't you comprehend that the male organisation is one and the female quite another? You seem to think it's merely an affair of clothes.

TESS: That's not what I'm saying!

DR MAUDSLEY: (*raising his voice startlingly*) Do not contradict me, miss! All you have demonstrated in your base and misguided outburst is that your sex has no capacity to control your emotional functions. (*Pause.*) Get out.

TESS: What?

DR MAUDSLEY: Out. And don't even think about coming back to a lecture of mine.

TESS *collects her belongings and leaves in silence.* MISS BOTT *tries to leave to follow her but* DR MAUDSLEY *begins again, quietly, dangerously.*

There comes a time, during a woman's public development, when she will expend tremendous energy in the recurring demands of menstruation. Can she bear mental drain in addition to these physical demands? The overexertion of a woman's brain, at the expense of other vital organs, may lead to atrophy, mania, or worse, may leave her incapacitated as a mother. These, sirs, are not opinions. They are facts of nature, proven by science.

(*To the* WOMEN.) I should throw the whole lot of you out.

In this extract and throughout the play you will notice that 'backslashes' (/) occur in the middle of lines. This is a theatrical convention used by some playwrights to indicate where one character begins talking over another. You will notice in this extract that Dr Maudsley does it to Tess often, but never the other way round. This gives a further clue, apart from what is being said, as to the opinions and status of the characters.

The first question

The first question requires you to imagine you are a performer in the play. A possible question might be:

> **3(a) There are specific choices in this extract for performers.**
>
> (i) You are going to play Tess. Explain one way you would use physical skills and one way you would use vocal skills to play this character in this extract.
> (4 marks)

For your response you will get one mark (✓) for each way identified and an additional mark (✓) for each linked explanation. Here are some ideas, but you wouldn't need them all – it's only a 4 mark question. To answer this you could focus on some of the following:

Physicality: Tess raises her hand; and then keeps it raised after she is ignored ✓ you could choose to register grim determination in your face ✓ even though the professor behaves as if you don't exist. Tess stands to address the room before she speaks in line 20 ✓: you should think about how quickly you might stand and whether you would speak directly to Dr Maudsley or look about at the other students ✓. In line 44, Tess admits to being agitated ✓: explain how you might show this in your physicality ✓. Think about what the physical manifestations might be of what Dr Maudsley describes in line 56 as a '*base and misguided outburst*' ✓.

At the end of the extract, Tess collects her belongings and leaves in silence ✓ There are physical choices here for the actor in how you walk out of the room – do you collect your things slowly and 'stalk' out with your head held high ✓, or do you leave cowed by your experience, hurried and small ✓?

Vocal skills: Tess' first speech causes '*consternation*' among the men. This might be because she stands with confidence and speaks out, unasked and loud into the room. You might take your time over what you have to say ✓, or rush through it, knowing that you are expressing yourself uninvited ✓.

When Maudsley talks about hysteria, perhaps you could choose to reflect that to some degree in your voice, becoming higher-pitched or speaking faster, taking quick snatched breaths – this is not, of course, because you are actually hysterical as he claims, but because of the nerves involved in debating with a person in authority ✓.

The second question

The 6 mark question also casts you as a performer, and might look like this:

> **3(a)(ii)** You are going to play Miss Bott. She is described as a chaperone in the cast list; she is a woman who accompanies the women when they are at lectures, and knits loudly. As a performer, give three suggestions of how you would use performance skills to convey her role during this extract. You must provide a reason for each suggestion. (6 marks)

COMPONENT 3: THEATRE MAKERS IN PRACTICE

To answer this you could focus on some of the following:

Use of **physicality**: Miss Bott has entered with Tess and other women before this extract begins, and has taken a seat to the side to knit ✓ in order to be seen but not interrupt ✓. Perhaps Miss Bott shows disapproval of Tess' actions through her facial expressions and increasingly louder knitting. Though she says nothing, actions speak louder than words. You might reflect your inner feelings in the speed and volume of your knitting – but are those feelings of disapproval or nerves and embarrassment? ✓

You must show Miss Bott's age and status by the manner in which she sits in her chair ✓ – is she a confident, bullish woman, or a mousey, awkward one? When Tess gathers her belongings and leaves, Miss Bott gets up to join her ✓, but Maudsley continues with his '*quiet, dangerous*' speech, so she sits back down ✓ too embarrassed to upset the great man further ✓.

The third question

The third, fourth and fifth questions ask you to imagine you are a director and then a designer working on the play. In order to prepare for this part of the exam you must have made all the production decisions you would make if you were indeed directing or designing it: it is not enough just to have got to know the text and made character or acting decisions.

Research past productions and have in mind a set design. Choose a form of stage layout from those explained on pages 10-11 of this book. You also need to know where people might be on the stage at key moments, entrances and exits, the position and style of any furniture, costumes, and so on. All decisions must be ones you know how to justify.

Context is extremely important. Make sure as part of your revision that you thoroughly research the context of both the time and place in which the play was written, and the time and place in which it is set. Try the search term 'blue stockings': the derogatory name for educated women of this period. The context will form the basis for some of your answers.

Here is an example of the third question:

3(b)(i) As a director, discuss how you would use one of the production elements below to bring this extract to life for your audience. You should make reference to the context in which the text was created and performed. (9 marks)

Choose one of the following:
- costume
- staging
- proxemics

In your response, if choosing **costume**, you could decide upon period costume of the late 1890s or a symbolic representation ✓. The men might be in shabby suits with short undergraduate gowns ✓; the ladies in long period skirts or dresses ✓. As students, they would not be particularly over dressed in a lecture hall ✓.

To show that he's senior to all, Dr Maudsley would be in a better suit and tie and with a full black academic gown ✓. Miss Bott might be in a sober, dark, unfussy dress and shawl, a little like the clothes favoured by Queen Victoria at this time, and carrying her knitting in a carpet bag ✓. A contemporary audience should draw the sense of period from the costume and accept the climate of male opinion as being of that time ✓.

Staging is another term for **blocking**; deliberate choices about where the performers stand and how they move on stage to communicate character relationships and plot, and to create interesting stage pictures in relation to the set, **props** and audience. To create the lecture hall, students would most likely sit on wooden chairs or benches, in rows ✓. The chair for Miss Bott needs to be '*to the side*' ✓, so as director you could choose to put her clearly in view on the opposite side to the students ✓ or at the back of them ✓ as long as she is visible throughout.

The door through which Tess is sent could be placed to maximise the dramatic effect of her exit ✓ and far enough away from Miss Bott to make it impossible for her to leave without disruption or embarrassment ✓. You need to know that in the original professional production, the play was performed on the **thrust stage** at Shakespeare's Globe Theatre, where the audience would have been on three sides of the stage ✓. The response from the close audience might have added to the sense of restriction in education for women ✓, however you could choose any form of staging for your production.

Blue Stockings at the Globe Theatre, 2013

Proxemics refer to the positions of characters in relation to each other and to the audience. Dr Maudsley might be raised higher than the students ✓ to reflect his status, and allow him to look down ✓ on Tess, particularly. Perhaps at the point where he draws attention to Tess showing hysterical signs, he might move very close to her ✓ in a challenging and quite threatening manner ✓.

The audience maintains some distance from the action ✓; this is not a scene requiring **direct address**. Similarly, the students would retain a respectful distance from Maudsley ✓. Miss Bott is the outsider who stays at the side ✓ despite wanting to move ✓. It might be particularly effective if she can distract without actually moving across the centre ✓.

The fourth question

This question also asks you to think from the perspective of a director:

> 3(b)(ii) Dr Maudsley, a renowned psychiatrist, has very high status in the play as a whole. As a director, discuss how the performer playing this role might demonstrate high status to the audience in this extract and the complete play.
> (12 marks)
>
> You must consider:
> - voice
> - physicality
> - stage space

COMPONENT 3: THEATRE MAKERS IN PRACTICE

In your response you must show an understanding of how a director works with a performer in a specific role within the given extract, but then you should also **link** this understanding to the whole text.

We see Dr Maudsley, in the extract and in the prologue, making long speeches which set out his views in a way that doesn't allow opposition. In each of his scenes in fact, Maudsley makes long, pompous speeches. How should these be received by the audience – in agreement, disbelief or anger?

His views are reflected in the beliefs and actions of the young men, particularly during the riot in act 2, scene 11 where the opinions turn to violence.

Consider the tone and style of Maudsley's speeches both when he is speaking out to a crowd and when he is talking individually to Tess and Mrs Welsh. Always give reasons for your statements, for example: Maudsley's intention is to appeal to the prejudice of the men ✓ and to irritate and belittle the women ✓.

In writing about use of **voice**, think about how the performer can use his voice to show authority ✓, dislike of contrary opinions ✓ and a certain arrogance in his belief that he's right, for example in

> (line 51) DR MAUDSLEY: Why can't you comprehend that the male organisation is one and the female quite another?

and, most telling of all,

> (line 55) DR MAUDSLEY: (raising his voice startlingly) Do not contradict me, miss!

Maudsley's entrance is built up, characters say '*he'll be here any minute,*' and, '*Sir, you are most welcome.*' The doors may be held open for him. All students stand as he enters and '*watch as this guru walks towards the front.*' In terms of **physicality**, Maudsley could play up the entrance, acknowledging audience and students with a nod and superior smile ✓.

Does he smile when he thinks he has won the discussion over Tess ✓? How does his face reflect his anger ✓ at the point of throwing her out? Could any of the young men copy his mannerisms ✓ to emphasise that they are his followers?

How does he stand when speaking ✓? Hands in his pockets to show nonchalant confidence and power ✓? Does he gesticulate and use arm movements ✓? Does he finger-point to drive home his views with force ✓?

Would he need personal props ✓ such as spectacles to take on and off? Does he need notes ✓ to speak from?

Thinking about **stage space**, If he's raised on a platform to speak does Maudsley ever come down to be close to Tess, perhaps to make her feel uncomfortable ✓? Does he focus some of his long speeches direct to the audience ✓ as if they too are students in need of his wisdom? Does he engage with them by coming closer physically ✓?

Does he sit in a chair on the platform at all ✓? Might he drink from a glass of water, for example, while Tess packs her things and leaves, before finishing his speech ✓? If so, does he do it sitting, standing on the platform or at the side of it ✓?

The fifth question

You will notice that each question has carried more marks than the one before, so you must write a little more for each answer. A final 14 mark question might look like this:

> 3(c) There are specific choices in this extract for designers.
>
> **Discuss how you would use one design element to enhance the production of this extract for the audience. (14 marks)**
>
> Choose one of the following:
> - Set
> - Lighting
> - Levels

To answer this kind of question, you have to show *how* the element you choose from the list would enhance enjoyment and understanding for the audience in a production of the extract on stage. What do you understand about production decisions the designer must make when working with the director to move this text from page to stage?

If you choose **set**, for example, you could discuss how the layout of the set, the separation of the rows of students ✓ (stage directions suggest that the women are in the front row) with the platform for Maudsley ✓ and chair for Bott ✓ makes the status and intention of each character clear ✓.

Why would the decision be made to raise Maudsley, to separate Miss Bott and to put Tess on the front row of students?

Is the design realistic with a lecture hall backdrop or symbolic with lighting and a few pieces of furniture?

How is the central tension between Tess and Maudsley heightened by the layout?

If you choose **lighting** you might discuss how lights enhance the atmosphere to create both mood and location. Explain what moods you want to create and how. Is the setting realistic? Is there light from above or through an upper window? Are there portraits on the wall of previous great scholars to be lit? Is the lecturer's platform spotlit? Is Miss Bott lit purposefully? Is there light from outside coming through the entrance/exit door?

If you choose **levels**, you could discuss how a tiered seating arrangement for the students may make the lecture hall more realistic, or, given the shortness of the scene, that may be too much. Budgetary considerations also may apply. A simple platform or podium for Maudsley may be enough, or could he be put in a pulpit as if he is preaching in a church?

Would there be benefit in having Miss Bott's chair on a higher level, or would that give her too much status, given the play's setting in the 1890s and women's place in society generally?

> **The stage layout and design pages of this book can help you in your decisions. Turn to pages 10-11 and 156-171. Researching previous productions is also an excellent source of inspiration.**

Dr Korczak's Example
by David Greig

The context of the play

David Greig became impressed by the life of Janusz Korczak (pronounced Kor-chock) a Polish-Jewish educator and writer of children's stories. There are parallels with Anne Frank – they were both victims of the Nazi holocaust and both kept diaries. Anne Frank couldn't escape death. Korczak had a chance, but didn't take it.

He was a forward-thinking man who in the 1930s was running progressive orphanages, founded the first national children's newspaper, and proposed children's courts and children's rights.

In 1942 the Nazis started to empty the ghetto they had forced Jews into, sending them on trains for 'resettlement in the east', which meant the death camp at Treblinka. Korczak was forced at gunpoint to lead with quiet dignity 200 orphans he'd taken care of to the trains.

Greig found an entry in Korczak's diary about having to expel a boy – Adzio – because his troublemaking brought police to the door which threatened other children.

The 'example' in the play comes in the questions it raises – should we resist violence peacefully or aggressively? Do we appeal to the good in people, or behave as badly as others?

A plot summary

During the war, as the Nazis occupied Europe, they confined Jews in Warsaw together in selected streets covering three and a half square kilometres, where 400,000 men, women and children were controlled as if in prison until 250,000 were transported to death camps in the summer of 1942.

The play tells the story of Dr Korczak and his orphanage within the Warsaw Ghetto. 'An orphanage is a community' at a time of great danger for Jewish people, children, the weak and anybody the Nazis wanted to destroy. Korczak is offered help and later a chance to escape, but stays with the children he cannot desert. Through characters played by actors, actors playing actors, and dolls representing the characters, we follow the final days of the orphanage and children.

The extensive use of dolls, not puppets, in the text is unusual and effective dramatically. They put some distance between the audience and the brutal facts of the murder of children, yet add an emotional energy on stage as audiences accept the dolls as characters, standing in for humans, telling the tragic story.

It's designed to make an audience think. It's not simply an anti-war play, it's more a study of man's inhumanity versus a single, shining beacon of hope and light in a dark world.

Greig's introduction explains his play very effectively, some of the writing process, how he developed the first idea and how watching his 4-year old daughter inspired the dolls which appear prominently in the play. He wrote that the dolls were 'respectful to the memory of Korczak's orphans because it would force the audience to inhabit the dolls imaginatively.'

The children of Janusz Korczak's orphanage

The characters

DR JANUSZ KORCZAK is the protagonist

ADZIO is a naughty child

STEPHANIE is an orphan girl who dislikes Adzio but gradually grows closer to him

STEPAN is Korczak's Christian friend who offers him false papers to escape

A PRIEST refuses permission for the orphans to use the church garden for 'air and green' as he is afraid of offending the Nazis

ACTRESS tells part of the story as an actress openly playing a character

ACTOR tells another part of the story in the role of an actor

TOM is a musician who is also mentioned as a character

CERNIAKOV is chairman of the Ghetto, the man allowed by the Nazis to run daily life there, before his last act is to lead all the Jews out for onward transmission to a concentration camp. He is offered special treatment for his good work. This character does not appear on Greig's cast list, but is as important as the others.

A note on page 8 explains how the play was written for three actors, that it has been performed with five and that experimenting with more is perfectly acceptable to the playwright. He also points out that his suggestions throughout for the use of the dolls are just that – ideas. He says each production company must 'create together a production style which integrates human actors with the use of dolls.'

Page to stage

The **actor's skills** include the bringing of characters to life, believably and credibly in often very short scenes, but also in this play to work with dolls (not puppets). The way the dolls are held, put into shapes or positions and the distance from the actors add to the message being conveyed by the play.

The **director's role** is to bring the separate actors' interpretations of their characters into a line that makes the play accessible to an audience. It is also to make the dolls work in a way that involves the audience without making them feel uncomfortable or reduced to humour.

The **designer's role** is to work with both director and actors to make each scene visually appropriate, to capture the place – the playground, Korczak's office, orphanage, dormitory, canteen, a street, Cerniakov's office and a cupboard, so that the audience is assisted in its journey through the performance.

Stage directions will assist you in understanding how the play is performed on stage, although in this play there are fewer directions than in many other plays.

Sample questions

As well as the question paper, you will get a source booklet with the extracts from each of the set texts on offer. You will only have studied one text, so find the extract you need in the source booklet and don't worry about the rest. The extract will be roughly 3 pages long in the source booklet and will link to roughly 4 pages from the copy of the text you are recommended to use in class.

In the question paper, the first line will say:

'You are involved in staging a production of this play. Please read the extract on page X of the source booklet.'

Look over the extract, which should be familiar to you from your study in class and your revision. Then begin to respond to the questions. It is recommended that you spend an hour on this section of the exam.

Remember: you are responding as a performer, director or designer. This is not English literature – it's Drama.

The sample questions on the next few pages relate to the following extract from pages 34-37 of the prescribed Capercaillie Press edition of *Dr Korczak's Example*. You will need to apply the suggestions made for the sample questions to the extract and questions you are given. If your preparation and understanding is good enough, it makes no difference whether you have practised the exact questions or not, you will be able to adapt.

Scene 9

    Afternoon. Dr Korczak's office.

STEPHANIE: Dr Korczak, you have a visitor.

    Stepan enters.

KORCZAK: Stepan! My friend. What are you doing here?

STEPAN: I bribed a guard at the gates of the Ghetto. I don't have
    long.

KORCZAK: Stepan, you're in danger. Christian Poles aren't
    allowed in the Ghetto. You can be shot.

STEPAN: I know Janusz. These are such dangerous times.
    I heard they'd put you in prison.

KORCZAK: Only for a week. I refused to wear their armband.

STEPAN: It must have been terrible.

KORCZAK: I enjoyed it.
    I had time to write.
    Time to tell stories.

STEPAN: This isn't a time for stories anymore.
    In the past things were less serious.
    Look — I have a false passport. I can get you out of the
    Ghetto.
    I can get you to Palestine.
    Please — save yourself.

KORCZAK: What about the children?

STEPAN: We can work something out — hide them with Polish
    families.
    Maybe we can hide them in the monasteries.

KORCZAC: I can't have the children locked in dark cellars always
    terrified of being discovered.

STEPAN: They might be safer than here.

KORCZAK: Can you guarantee their safety?

STEPAN: Of course not. I can't guarantee my own safety.

KORCZAK: I can't leave the children.

STEPAN: You must.

KORCZAK: I can't abandon them.
    I don't want to.
    It would be desertion.
    They've all been deserted by their parents.
    I can't do that to them again.

STEPAN: The Nazis are tightening a noose around you.
    You have a chance to escape.
    You're an important man.
    I beg you to take it.

KORCZAK: No.
    Tell me Stepan, when you came here, did you think I would

                Say yes to your plan?
STEPAN: No.
    They embrace.
KORCZAK: They won't kill us.
    Life will be hard,
    but they won't kill us.
    We must carry on. We must show them how to live.
    That's how we fight them, Stepan. Every time a Christian like
    you embraces a Jew like me we're fighting back.
    Stepan leaves.

Scene 10
    STEPHANIE returns carrying a clipboard.
STEPHANIE: I have the court cases for the week, Dr Korczak.
KORCZAK: Thank you Stephanie, put them on my desk.
STEPHANIE: There's a new case. Just in this morning.
    Korczak reads.
KORCZAK: Oh dear. Adzio.
STEPHANIE: Bruno says Adzio stole his bread in the night.
    Bruno's furious. He was saving the bread for his kid brother.
    I told you he was rough.
KORCZAK: Very well.
    We'll hold the court this afternoon.
    ADZIO bursts in.
ADZIO: Hey boss, one of the kids told me I've got to go to some
    court thing.
KORCZAK: Bruno says you stole his bread.
ADZIO: And you believe him?
KORCZAK: The court will decide, on the evidence.
ADZIO: I'm not scared of a bunch of kids.
KORCZAK: A children's court might seem strange to you now
    Adzio.
    But I promise you, in fifty years' time, when you're an old
    man, every school, every children's home will have one.
    A child has a right to be judged by people his own age.
ADZIO: If you think I stole the mongrel's bread why don't you
    Just give me a whipping?
KORCZAK: Because I believe in justice.
ADZIO: There's a German with a gun out there.
    Put him in your court.
    See what happens.
    You got a gun too?
    Who cares about your court?
ADZIO exits.

Note: Treat the two scenes as one, as they are both set in Korczaks' office.

The first question

The first question requires you to imagine you are a performer in the play. A possible question might be:

> **6(a)** There are specific choices in this extract for performers.
>
> (i) You are going to play Adzio. Explain one way you would use vocal skills and one way you would use physical skills to play this character in this extract. (4 marks)

For your response you will get one mark (✓) for each way identified and an additional mark (✓) for each linked explanation. Here are some ideas, but you wouldn't need them all – it's only a 4 mark question. To answer this you could focus on some of the following:

Vocal tone: Adzio enters with a statement that may express surprise ✓ that he has to go to a court, or it could be aggression ✓. When he says

    (line 64) ADZIO: I'm not scared of a bunch of kids.

It could be said loud with bravado ✓, or perhaps whispered in a menacing way ✓, or even with a tremor which indicates that he is in fact a little scared after all ✓. His question why he doesn't just get a whipping could be sly ✓, knowing that Korczak wouldn't whip him ✓. At the mention of justice, Adzio points out, perhaps loud and angrily ✓ that the German with a gun should be put in a court; he's taunting Korczak here ✓.

Physicality: Stage directions indicates that Adzio 'bursts in', suggesting speed and energy in his physicality ✓ He might stay still **centre stage** through the section until beginning to pace about agitatedly ✓ at the mention of the German with a gun. Perhaps you think he might approach Korczak ✓ on the line about the whipping, in order to provoke him more ✓. Finally, his exit could be in triumph or stubbornness, or genuinely he might not care about the court, with a shrug, a rude gesture or a defiant look.

The second question

The 6 mark question also casts you as a performer, and might look like this:

> **6(a)(ii)** You are going to play Stepan. He is welcomed as Korczak's friend and is clearly a man of influence outside the Ghetto. As a performer, give three suggestions of how you would use performance skills to show his concern for Korczak from the start of this extract. You must provide a reason for each suggestion. (6 marks)

To answer this you could focus on some of the following:

Use of **space** and **physicality**: hugging Korczak on entry and greeting him warmly ✓ to show they are friends ✓; coming close when talking about the false passport ✓ in case anyone is listening ✓; moving away ✓, irritated with your friend on the line

    (line 28) STEPAN: Of course not, I can't guarantee my own safety.

COMPONENT 3: THEATRE MAKERS IN PRACTICE

and closer again ✓ when begging Korczak to escape, to make the appeal stronger ✓. When you depart, you might choose to embrace him again ✓ because you are still friends ✓, but exit with disappointment, perhaps slowly and with downcast eyes ✓ because you had hoped to talk sense into Korczak ✓.

Use of **voice**: You would have a sense of urgency and speak fast ✓ when talking about bribing the guard, because you don't have long ✓; you might drop your voice ✓ on '*I have a false passport*' to keep it secret in the room ✓; but use an encouraging tone ✓ on '*I can get you to Palestine*', because you know that that would appeal to Korczak ✓.

You would also be upbeat in your assurance that you can work something out for the children ✓, as that is Korczak's concern and you wish to alleviate it and encourage him to accept your offer of help ✓. However, your tone may change to irritation, and you may even raise your voice a little ✓ in saying that you can't make a guarantee.

The urgency in your voice might return ✓ when you say

    (line 36) STEPAN: The Nazis are tightening a noose around you.

And finally desperation shows through when you '*beg*' him ✓, as you've run out of other persuasive techniques.

The third question

The third, fourth and fifth questions ask you to imagine you are a director and then a designer working on the play. In order to prepare for this part of the exam you must have made all the production decisions you would make if you were indeed directing or designing it: it is not enough just to have got to know the text and made character or acting decisions.

Research past productions and have in mind a set design. Choose a form of stage layout from those explained on pages 10-11 of this book. You also need to know where people might be on the stage at key moments, entrances and exits, the position and style of any furniture, costumes, and so on. All decisions must be ones you know how to justify.

Context is extremely important. Make sure as part of your revision that you thoroughly research the context of both the time and place in which the play was written, and the time and place in which it is set. Try the search term 'Warsaw ghetto'. The context will form the basis for some of your answers.

Here is an example of the third question:

> **6(b)(i) As a director, discuss how you would use one of the production elements below to bring this extract to life for your audience. You should make reference to the context in which the text was created and performed. (9 marks)**
>
> Choose one of the following:
> - costume
> - staging
> - proxemics

When I am Little Again by Yevgeny Ibragimov also told the story of Janusz Korczak using dolls. This production was performed in St Petersburg in 2015

The question asks you to refer to the context in which the text was created and performed – originally for secondary school students. Greig's intention was to present Korczak, his beliefs and work in the face of oppression. In this scene he is doing that despite Adzio's behaviour.

To answer, you could focus on some of the following:

If choosing **costume** you might decide upon 1930s period clothes ✓, remembering that the orphans generally were poor, ragged and often in found clothes too big or too small ✓. Adzio and Stephanie are Jewish and their costumes would reflect their culture ✓. Modern footwear should be avoided; Adzio could even be barefoot ✓.

Dr Korczak could be in a warm suit with a waistcoat and plain tie ✓, which shows his superior status, his age and his desire to maintain some conventions as head of an institution ✓. Stepan, equal in social status, would be dressed similarly ✓.

If writing about **staging**, you need to concentrate on **blocking**; deliberate choices about where the performers stand and how they move on stage to communicate character relationships and plot, and to create interesting stage pictures in relation to the set, **props** and audience. Audience sightlines are important, particularly if you are imagining the play in a non-**proscenium arch** layout.

If you discuss **proxemics** you will receive a mark each for explaining the distances between the adults and the children, the speaking adults, the relative status of each character, and the space between performers and audience to make it more intimate or less. The confined space and the way in which the performers fill it can say a good deal about what the director's intentions are, and affect how the audience respond to the tension in the scene.

COMPONENT 3: THEATRE MAKERS IN PRACTICE

The fourth question

This question also asks you to think from the perspective of a director:

> **6(b)(ii)** Korczak is the character with the highest status within the orphanage throughout the play. As a director, discuss how the performer playing this role might demonstrate high status to the audience in this extract and the complete play. (12 marks)
>
> You must consider:
>
> voice
>
> physicality
>
> stage space

In your response you must show an understanding of how a director works with a performer in a specific role within the given extract, but then you should also **link** this understanding to the whole text.

You should focus on how director and actor work together to interpret the role which requires status, responsibility and authority, while being subject to the higher power of the Nazis. You should refer to the extract but also show understanding of the full play, and give reasons to support the specific examples you choose. The audience must always be your main focus: what does the director intend them to feel at particular moments?

You could write about Korczak's use of **voice**. When dealing with Adzio, Stepan, Cerniakov and the Nazi officer, he changes in tone; but he also maintains his quiet reasonableness throughout, despite what he may be thinking; his tone changes when making the announcement about the flies to be killed, and when playing the slave game with Adzio through the dolls. How do each of these things make his status clear to the audience?

Korczak's **physicality** also helps to portray a man of authority forced to obey the Nazis. When he is called a '*mad old monkey*' he finds it funny – think about how his physicality might tie in to this; he is patient when explaining the virtues of the court to Adzio, and his calm nature can be expressed through his movements. After the church stone throwing incident in scene 19 he is described as putting 'his head in his hands', 'tired and depressed.'

There is a quiet dignity in his carrying a child in one arm and the flag in the other as he leads the children to the train in scene 24.

In terms of **stage space**, much of the play sees Korczak in an office: this is his domain and he is comfortable in it, the audience should feel this and it enhances his status. His interaction with stage furniture such as his desk and chair, and props such as the gavel, should be confident and assured. A performer can give him a flow around the stage that reflects his personality: being in quiet control, observant, compassionate and caring. The court scene is also in the office, but the use of the dolls prevents it being overcrowded. Korczak is one of the manipulators of the dolls to support the action, so he should maintain his flow while doing that as well as speaking. He is also seen outside, where he has an understated confidence, a conviction that his ideas are right and time will prove him correct.

The fifth question

You will notice that each question has carried more marks than the one before, so you must write a little more for each answer. A final 14 mark question might look like this:

> **3(c) There are specific choices in this extract for designers.**
>
> **Discuss how you would use one design element to enhance the production of this extract for the audience. (14 marks)**
>
> Choose one of the following:
> - Set
> - Lighting
> - Levels

To answer this you should focus on how the designer uses the elements to improve the experience for the audience and make the play accessible.

If you choose the **set**, it's in Korczak's office, which may be small and cramped or totally sparse ✓. There could be shelves with little on them ✓. The desk and chairs may be shabby and ill-matching ✓. There could be more than one door, or perhaps if there is only one it would enhance the sense of claustrophobia brought about by the German guard outside ✓. There may be a window through which Adzio spots the German with a gun, or it could be totally windowless ✓. In each case you must remark upon how the choice you've made would enhance the production for the audience.

If you choose to write about **lighting**, it could be quite gloomy, even during the day ✓. The moods change in the office, so changing light levels and colours could reflect those ✓. When the door opens, does light come in from outside ✓? If your production is to be slightly less naturalistic, might Stepan and Korczak be spotlit while whispering secretly together ✓?

The office could be on one **level**, or a higher level could be made on which sits the desk ✓, to enhance Korczak's status ✓ when he is sitting behind or on it.

> **The stage layout and design pages of this book can help you in your decisions. Turn to pages 10-11 and 156-171. Researching previous productions is also an excellent source of inspiration.**

Live Theatre Evaluation

Section B of the written paper is the live theatre evaluation part. Section B is worth 15 marks – a good deal fewer than section A. You should spend 30 minutes on this section. There will be two questions and you must answer both based on the performance you have seen.

This is the part of the exam that you can take in notes for. You can only have 500 words, plus sketches, so the notes must be carefully prepared before the date of the exam so that they are useful and clear.

Why are we asked to do a live theatre evaluation?

Understanding how and why a production is effective is a key skill to learn over the duration of the course. It can make going to see future productions even more enjoyable. You will need to demonstrate in the exam that you can offer informed and critical writing in response to the questions.

You don't have to have the same opinions as everyone else in your class, as your teacher, or as a professional theatre critic. You do however need to be able to defend and justify your opinions with relevant examples that are analysed, not simply described.

Choosing what to see for your live theatre evaluation

It is likely, but not always the case, that you will see the theatre piece you are going to evaluate in the exam with your classmates as part of a school trip.

It does not matter if you see a piece on your own instead, however, if you do and your teacher or class hasn't seen it, then they may not be able to help you in the preparations so effectively.

You need to see a piece that will offer you enough to write about in the exam. Make sure you are seeing something that will have set, costumes, music or sound and lighting alongside the acting. While seeing a minimalist production might be very interesting, it wouldn't give you a great deal to write about in the exam.

Lighting in *The Woman in Black*, Fortune Theatre, London

There are restrictions on what you MUST NOT use as an example:

You cannot write about something that you have not seen live yourself, i.e. you must be in the audience at the performance in the same venue. Only if there are extreme extenuating circumstances are you allowed to use a live theatre broadcast such as an 'NT Live' production seen in the cinema as an example, and your school or examination centre would have to apply for special consideration if this were the case.

GCSE DRAMA STUDY GUIDE

You are not to use a performance that is sung through in its entirety. In theory, this does allow you to use a musical as an example, as long as there are scenes of acting in between the musical numbers. However, if choosing this style of performance you have to consider carefully whether a musical has enough acting between songs for you to talk about should the question require you to discuss this.

Does it need to be a play I have studied?

There are no rules saying you have to use a play you have studied. In fact, if you know nothing about what you are going to see before the trip in terms of a plot, themes, characters, design and so on, then you will be able to enjoy the performance without lots of pre-conceived ideas.

On the other hand, try not to get too caught up in the plot, or overwhelmed by the whole spectacle to notice the technical and directorial decisions that have been made.

Things to look out for

There are lots of things you should be looking out for in the performance. On the next few pages, spider diagrams or mind maps will give you key words to think about when you're watching it:

Acting mind map:
- Use of proxemics
- Body language
- Posture
- Gait
- Eye contact
- Status
- Facial expression
- Age
- Movement
- Use of voice
  - Volume
  - Accent
  - Pitch
  - Pause
  - Tone
  - Pace
  - Emphasis
- Characterisation
- Communication / interaction with others on stage
- Gesture

Though productions may be filled with amazing design, it is still the acting that carries much of the weight of the performance's success. The actors have the main job of communicating the meaning of the play. How they do this and how successful you judge them to be is what you analyse if the question is on acting.

LIVE THEATRE EVALUATION

Costume

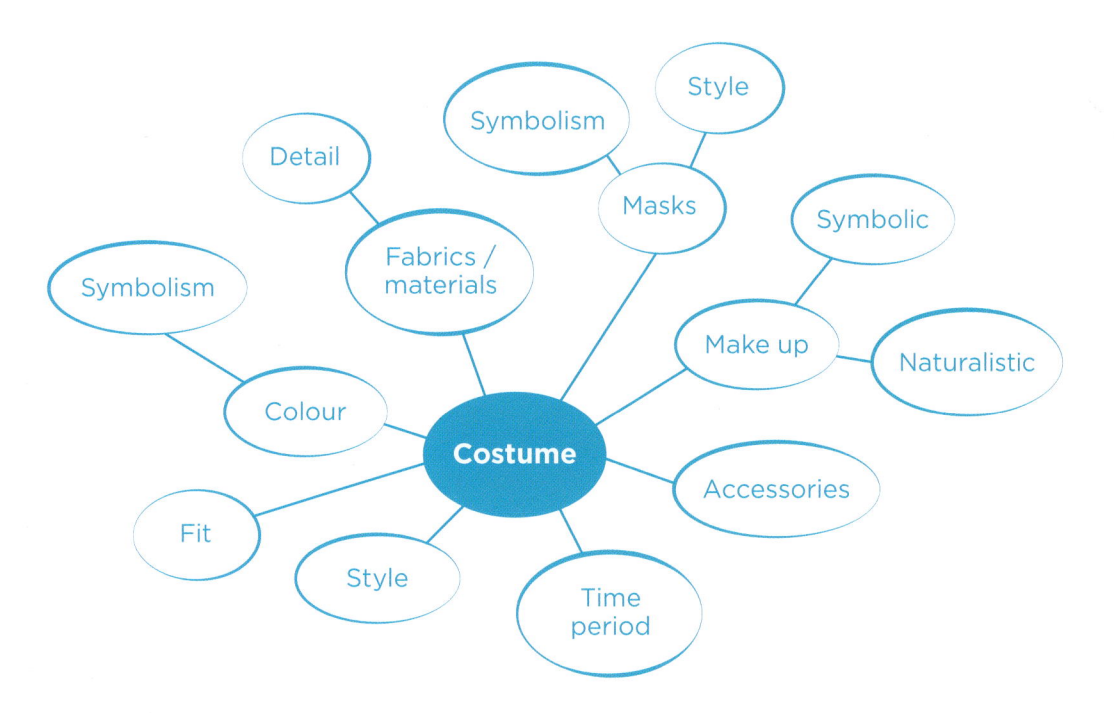

- Detail
- Symbolism
- Style
- Symbolism
- Fabrics / materials
- Masks
- Symbolic
- Make up
- Naturalistic
- Colour
- Accessories
- Fit
- Style
- Time period

Costume plays a huge part in helping us to interpret character. It can tell us about their age, class or status, era and maybe it might have some hidden symbolism revealing an inner nature to the character. From the performance you see, pick key examples; put them into your notes using the key words above to help you describe and analyse.

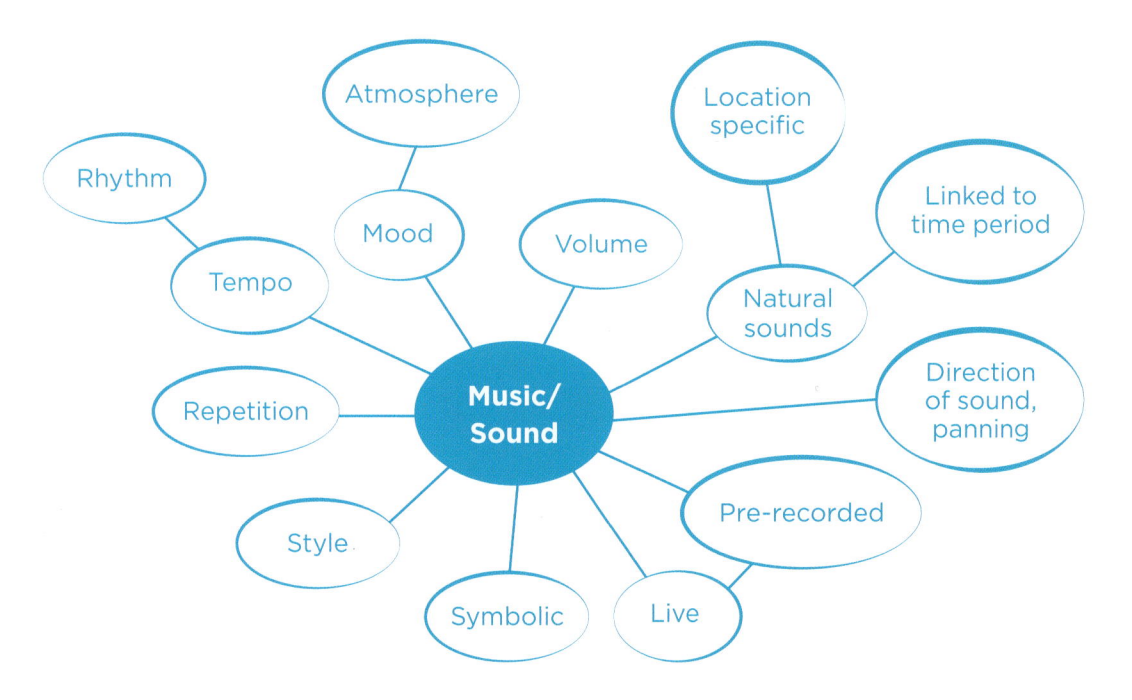

Music/Sound

- Atmosphere
- Location specific
- Rhythm
- Mood
- Volume
- Linked to time period
- Tempo
- Natural sounds
- Repetition
- Direction of sound, panning
- Style
- Pre-recorded
- Symbolic
- Live

Sound effects and music can be informed by the text or plot, or they can be abstract – to create mood or tension, for example. The choice whether to use live or pre-recorded sound is a big design decision, as is sometimes where the sound comes from. In *The Woman in Black*, a long running stage-thriller, sound often came from speakers surrounding the audience, to make them feel that they were in the centre of the action.

GCSE DRAMA STUDY GUIDE

THINGS TO LOOK OUT FOR

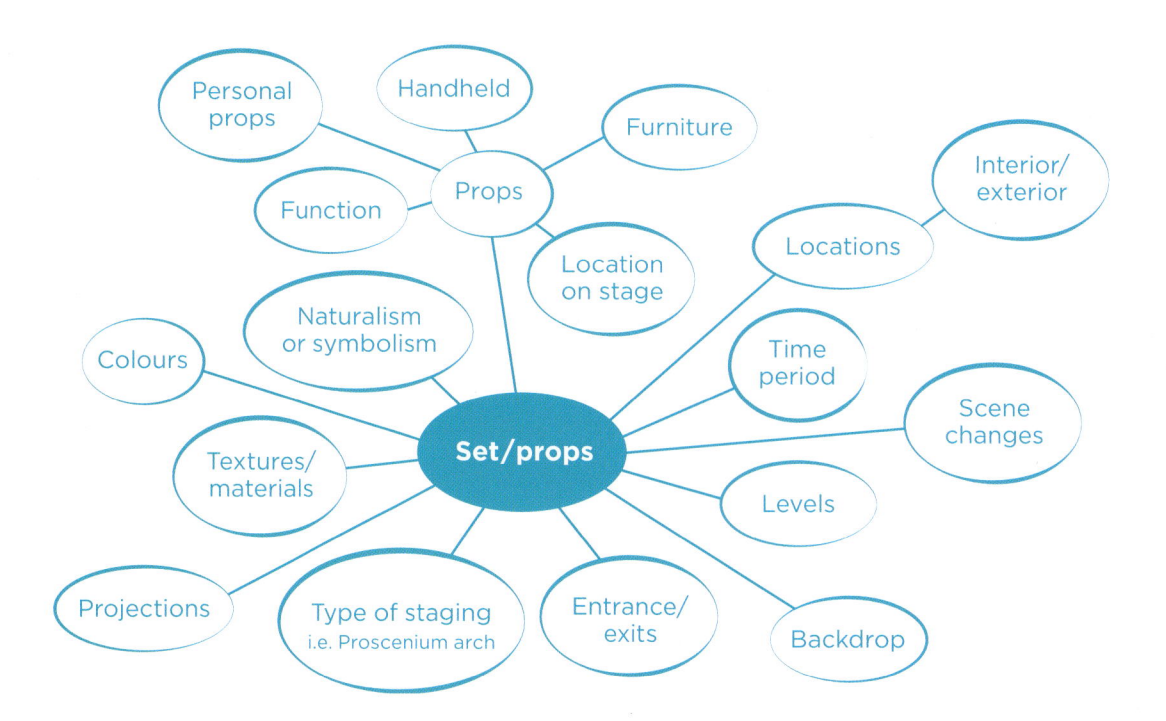

Set/props mind map:
- Props
  - Personal props
  - Handheld
  - Furniture
  - Function
  - Location on stage
- Locations
  - Interior/exterior
- Time period
- Scene changes
- Levels
- Backdrop
- Entrance/exits
- Type of staging i.e. Proscenium arch
- Projections
- Textures/materials
- Colours
- Naturalism or symbolism

You might also consider whether the space in which the performance is taking place has an effect on the production. To use the example of *The Woman in Black*, again, London performances have taken place in a small Victorian theatre – adding to the intimate feeling of the production and creating a ghostly atmosphere even before the play starts.

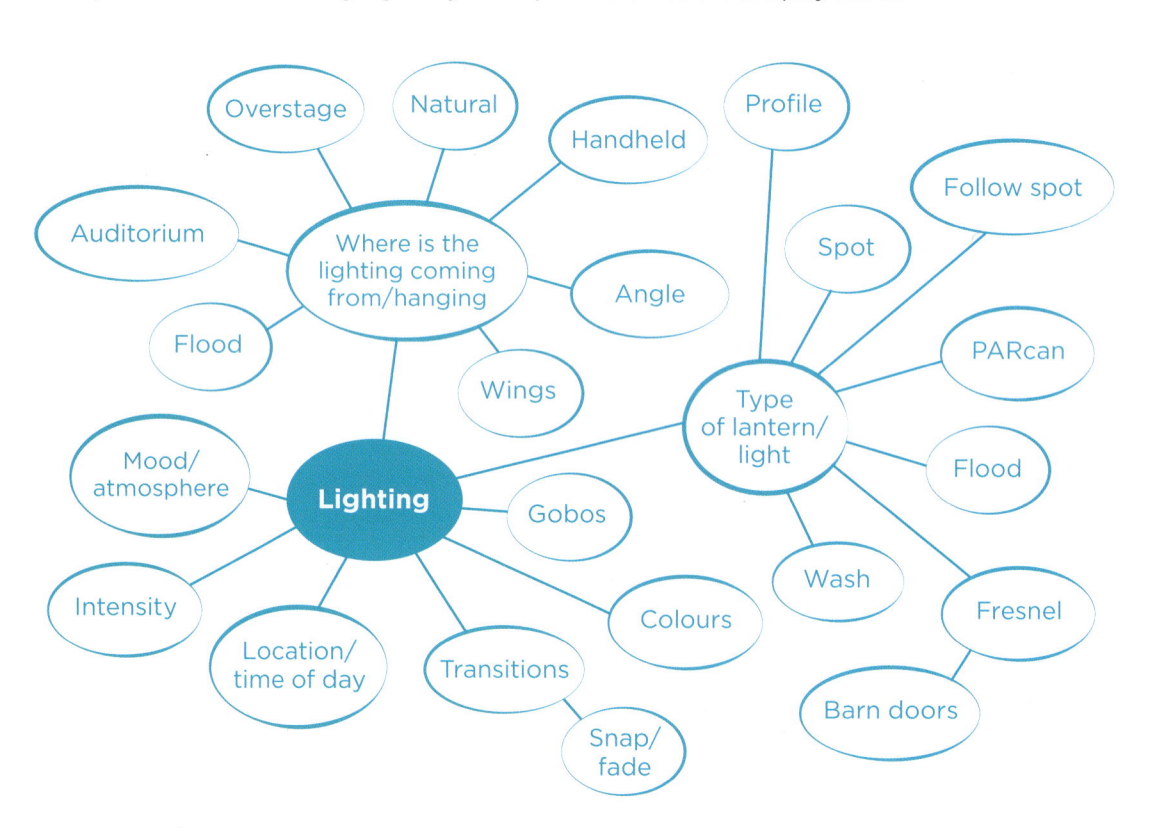

Lighting mind map:
- Where is the lighting coming from/hanging
  - Overstage
  - Natural
  - Handheld
  - Auditorium
  - Flood
  - Wings
  - Angle
- Type of lantern/light
  - Profile
  - Follow spot
  - Spot
  - PARcan
  - Flood
  - Fresnel
  - Barn doors
  - Wash
- Gobos
- Colours
- Transitions
  - Snap/fade
- Location/time of day
- Intensity
- Mood/atmosphere

Lighting can play a very active part in a performance. It can enhance a set or highlight an actor, and it can change a mood or atmosphere. Pages 160-163 of this book can help you to understand more about the types of lighting, angles, effects and considerations for a designer, which in turn will help you to interpret and write about what you saw in the live theatre piece.

Overall, pages 156-171 of this book will help you to understand what impact design might have on a production, so that you can decide what effect it had on the one you saw.

After the trip

You must make notes as soon as possible after seeing the show. The best thing to do is to put everything down under key headings. Don't worry about word restrictions at this stage – just get it onto the paper while it is fresh in your mind. You can then refine and edit later on.

In your notes, have examples which consider:

- Performers and acting
- Design considerations including costume, set, lighting, sound/music – use the spider diagrams to help you with key words to mention
- The director's concept or interpretation, and the chosen performance style
- Impact in key moments and how this was achieved – this could involve layering different elements. At a key moment, what effect did the combination of set, costume, lighting, acting and sound produce?
- The use of the space
- How ideas were communicated during the performance – again, this could involve layering different elements

Refining the notes for the exam

Have clear headings that work for you. The 500 word allowance for the notes means that you will not be able to write prepared responses; the exam is not simply about copying from your notes. In the exam you will have to build your response, using your notes to prompt you.

How do I revise?

Have a go at practice questions to maintain your ability to respond under timed conditions and pressure. Later, read over practice question responses that you have done previously, aiming to understand why you got the marks that you did from your teacher, and looking for ways to improve, or to repeat successes. Look at exemplars from others that you have been given, that are available in this book, or directly from the exam board.

On the day

Ensure you have the notes with you, that you know the number of questions to answer, and how long to spend on each section of the exam: an hour on section A and half an hour on section B.

Eat a good breakfast. Have at least one spare pen with you. Arrive ahead of the start time.

In the exam, read the question more than once to be sure you understand it. It can be useful to write down a plan or to highlight on your notes what you are going to write about. Stick to timings once you are underway. Read the question again at some point once you have begun writing, to ensure you are still on track with your response.

Analyse, don't just describe.

The paper begins by asking you to

Write the title, venue and date of the performance you have seen in the space below.

Performance details

Title:

Venue:

Date seen:

There are then two questions – you must answer both.

Sample question

> 9(a) Analyse how lighting was used at one key moment during the production. (6 marks)

You should have key moments in mind for each design element. Here pick as an example the one you think you can describe and then analyse the best. Outline the moment using the language of drama: lots of the key words in the glossary at the back of this book might be of use to you. Be as brief as you can about the plot in respect of the example you pick; your ability to talk about the plot is not going to gain you marks but you may need to outline what was going on in the story to give the example a context. Use the spider diagram or headings in your notes to help with key words.

For example:

> The actor playing the Young Kipps was acting as if asleep in Eel Marsh House. He was downstage with this area dimly lit in a sepia wash. The colour reminded me of an old faded photograph, which linked to the fact this was an old memory of Kipps'. The dim lighting with the Young Kipps asleep was quite soothing, until the sound of the rocking chair began, again, quietly at first and then louder. This woke the sleeping Kipps, whose head shot up and he gasped, making us all jump. The dim lighting no longer seemed calming now, instead it seemed threatening and as if it might hide things – such as The Woman in Black. He then lit a candle, this created eerie shadows against the gauze and he walked off stage right which left us in darkness with nothing visible on stage for a moment, and the sepia wash went off – we were alone in the dark which added to the tension of the moment...

LIVE THEATRE EVALUATION

Another question might be:

> 9(b) Evaluate how music and/or sound was used to enhance the production and create impact for the audience. Give specific examples to support your response. (9 marks)

Here you might say that some moments were more successful than others – negative criticism is allowed, as long as it, as with everything else, is justified. You must consider the audience and specify what the impact was for you. Did the music change the mood, did a sound create surprise for the audience, did it set the scene?

Everything that was suggested for the 6 mark question also applies in your response here.

For example:

> Sound effects were used frequently to create a picture in the mind of the audience and move the plot along to different locations, which was highly effective especially as there was little set. For example, when the Young Kipps was travelling with Keckwick to Eel Marsh House, they did so on a pony and trap. There was no horse and cart on stage, however. Instead the actors sat on the wicker basket and jiggled side to side as if rocked by the motion of the moving cart. The sound effects were key in completing the mental picture and firing my imagination: the sounds were of the 'clip clop' of the horse's hooves and the trundle of the wheels over the ground. The sound was calming, lulling me into a false sense of ease...

TOP TIPS
- Analyse, don't just describe.
- When you do describe, remember the examiner may well not have seen the production, and even if they have, they are expecting your description to be clear.
- Don't offer lengthy explanations of the plot or narrative.
- Make sure you are certain what the question is asking you before you start writing.
- Don't just copy from your notes – apply the notes and your understanding to the specifics of the question.

Thinking about Working as a Designer?

GCSE Drama does not have to be all about acting. You may be interested in working as a designer for all or some of the components of the course. This section is intended to help you decide whether the design route is a good option for you, and what skills you might need to succeed.

WHY IS DESIGN IMPORTANT?

All theatre productions contain an element of design. A good design can pull all the elements of a production together and is as important as the acting or the script. A successful design can help an audience really to imagine the location where a play is set, whether through brightness and colour of light, or through the type of music and its volume level at the end of a scene. Costumes give the audience an immediate impression of a character, while set design helps to transport us away from the theatre space into a scene's location.

Working as a designer can be a hugely rewarding and creative process and might suit those of you who either don't like to be in the spotlight all the time, or who have interests beyond drama in art, music, fashion, IT or other practical activities such as model making.

How does design fit into the GCSE course?

Design roles in each component work as follows:

Component 1: **Devising** – a designer will create a design (costume, set, lighting or sound) for the devised piece along with a portfolio about the design process.

Component 2: Performance from Text – a designer will create a design for two extracts from a set play.

Component 3: **Theatre Makers in Practice** (written exam) – this exam paper contains questions which ask you to focus on your ideas for design for your studied play in section A, and it is possible you will be asked to write about effective designs that you have seen on the stage in section B: Live Theatre Evaluation.

If you decide that you would like to go down the design route then it's important to check that your school or college has the following minimum resources available (more specific details follow on pages 156-171):

- Lighting board and 3 different types of lantern
- Suitable materials or budget for costume and set
- A mixing desk and two types of microphone.

THINKING ABOUT WORKING AS A DESIGNER?

What kind of designer should I be?

Costume

Costume design includes working with fabrics and colour, drawing and researching ideas, and attending rehearsals to see how costumes will be used.

What kind of person might be good at costume?
- Someone creative who is interested in clothing and fashion
- Someone who is interested in drawing and painting
- Someone who is tactful and can get on well with others – actors often feel anxious about costumes, and designers will need to be able to persuade and reassure!

Lighting

Design work will include drawing ground plans, computer work, and supervision of the rigging of lights.

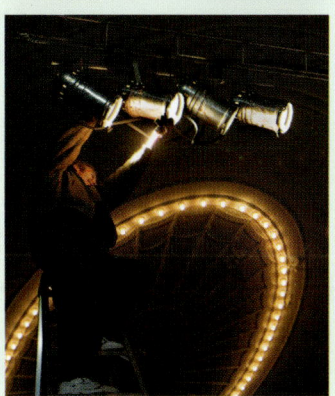

What kind of person would be good at lighting?
- Someone organised, logical and good at planning their time
- Someone computer literate
- Someone who's good at physics and/or interested in photography.

Set

Set design involves drawing ground plans and research including telephone research to source materials or hire elements of the set.

What kind of person might be good at set design?
- Someone who is good with measurements and spatial awareness – mathematicians often make good set designers!
- Someone who is happy to talk on the phone to hire companies and who can explain clearly what they require and perhaps be persuasive – often drama departments in schools have very little budget for design!
- Someone who is practical and who likes to build, paint or make things.

Sound

Sound design involves choosing and recording sound effects and music, working on the computer and spending time in rehearsal to check what sound is required.

What kind of person might be good at sound design?
- Someone who is interested in music (not necessarily a musician)
- Someone competent at using a computer – Apple Mac computers are ideal for sound design
- Someone who is interested in sound and how it can create different moods and atmospheres. Often film addicts make good sound designers!

Working as a costume designer

Over the next few pages we will look at the role of a costume designer, and the specific requirements for the different parts of your GCSE course should you wish to be assessed in this role.

What does a costume designer do?

A costume designer's main job is to help to tell the story of the play visually by the costumes that they design. They need to create costumes that fit in with the style of the play as a whole and also make sure that the costumes themselves will work on the stage – can the actor actually act in the costume or does it restrict their movement, for example?

A costume designer needs to be able to work well with the director of the play but also with the other designers such as lighting and set. This is to make sure that everyone is working to the same style and has the same dramatic intentions. For example, a costume designer and set designer may decide to use a similar palette of colours for their designs, and a lighting designer would need to know about this to enable the designing of lighting states. It's important to collaborate, for example a set designer must make sure that there is enough space on the set for the costumes (there have been cases where costumes won't fit through the doorways of a set!)

So, for your GCSE what do **you** need to do as a costume designer? Let's look at the specifics of what you need to do before exploring how to go about it:

Component 1: Devising

- Produce two costume designs for two characters, incorporating hair, make up and masks if appropriate (this will depend very much on the style and theme of your devised play).
- Also produce a **costume plot** or list of costumes/accessories worn by each performer which shows any changes in costume (we'll look at how to do this later in the chapter).
- Supervise the making or sourcing of the costumes. It's important to remember that you don't have to make the costume yourself – you can supervise someone else doing it or you can hire elements of it. So don't panic if you and the sewing machine don't exactly get on.
- Realise the costume designs in performance – this is the bit where you can look with pride at all your hard work as the actor wears your brilliantly designed costume!

Portfolio

Along with your practical work you need to keep a portfolio which is worth 45 marks. Your portfolio can be made up of notes, research, sketches, photographs and so on just like a designer's notebook.

You must also answer the following questions:

- What was your initial response to the stimuli and what were the intentions of the piece?
- What work did your group do in order to explore the stimuli and start to create ideas for performance?
- What were some of the significant moments during the development process and when rehearsing and refining your work?
- How did you consider **genre**, structure, character, form, style, and language throughout the process?
- How effective was your contribution to the final performance?
- Were you successful in what you set out to achieve?

THINKING ABOUT WORKING AS A DESIGNER?

Component 2: Performance from Text

To work as a costume designer for this unit you need to do the following:

- If working as a costume designer on both extracts you must have two final costume designs for two characters, incorporating hair, make up and masks if appropriate.
- Produce a **costume plot** or list of costumes/accessories worn by each performer which shows any changes in costume.
- Supervise the making or the sourcing of your two costumes. If you are sourcing (finding) rather than making it is important that you have designed the costume first – you cannot be assessed for a costume that you have just found; it must be sourced to your design.
- Realise your costumes in performance.

If you decide to work as a costume designer for one extract and then a performer for the second extract you only need to present **one** costume design for assessment rather than two. Your costume plot should still cover all the other costumes required for the extracts.

Where to start

If you are designing costumes for a devised play (component 1) then you need to spend lots of time in rehearsals as the play develops. This is so that you can work collaboratively with the rest of your group, and you know what your costumes need to be used for.

Ask the following questions:

- Where is the play set?
- Do we want the costumes to match the era when the play is set? (You can of course change a play's setting to something more modern – often this can be quite an exciting task for a costume designer.)
- Colour is very important so think about what colours you want to use and why? (consider themes in the play – can you show these through colour, such as red for danger or passion?)
- What do the actors need to be able to do in the costumes? (Watch what they're doing and keep this in mind as you design.)

If you are designing for component 2 then you need to read and study the play from which your extracts come. Again, ask the questions above. Then, you are able to make a list of each character, what they wear (costumes and accessories) and whether they need more than one costume. This is your **costume plot**.

> Search for **costume plots** online and you will find a variety of images which you might use as templates to make sure you have all the information covered.

Style and period

Remember that as a costume designer you are not being expected to design something that is historically accurate for the stage. It is more important that your costume shows an awareness of the actor's body and how they need to use it when playing the part. Often the choice of fabric is the most important part of designing a costume as different fabrics can sit very differently depending on their weight. You don't want to clothe your actor in a fabric so heavy that she can't move or breathe for being too hot!

There are lots of books and online articles on costume design and history of costume.

GCSE DRAMA STUDY GUIDE

Have a look at these to get a sense of the period of your play but remember that you're not being asked to recreate history – often some modern fashions contain an element of historical clothing (such as a modern trend for military jackets) so try to use alternatives where possible. When Alison Chitty designed a costume for Cleopatra played by Judi Dench in 1987 she used a sari fabric rather than something traditionally Egyptian so that she could design an outfit of more subtle colours and loose flowing fabric which suited her actor's style and body shape.

Inspiration and research

There are lots of ways to inspire yourself when designing costumes. Try some of the following:

- Create a **mood board** of colours using cut outs from magazines and samples of fabrics (some shops will give away offcuts if you ask nicely).

Judi Dench in *Antony and Cleopatra*, National Theatre, 1987

Costume design drawings by Isaac Lummis for *Showtime*, Victorian State Schools Spectacular in Melbourne, Australia, 2011

THINKING ABOUT WORKING AS A DESIGNER?

- Study costume history books and articles online to get a feel for where your play is set.

Working with others

Much of a costume designer's work involves collaboration with others, so it's really important to be able to get along and work well with your team. It's particularly important that the actors trust you and feel comfortable with you – they are then more likely to want to wear the costumes that you design for them.

Don't

- Talk about body measurements with any of your cast in public (most people don't want their measurements broadcast to others!)
- Ask your actors to try on a costume and then immediately show everyone else – you need to talk to them first about their feelings before everyone else gets involved.

Do

- Encourage your actors to wear 'practise' clothes in rehearsal. For example, if you know that they'll be wearing a long dress, try to get them to rehearse in one. This will make things easier for them and for you.
- Listen to your actors about what they feel comfortable wearing – never make them wear something they feel unsure about, as this might affect their performance (and yours).

Health and safety

In all of your written work you will be required to show that you have taken notice of health and safety concerns. These might include:

Rehearsal room:

- Make sure that actors' clothing is not too long for them – you don't want them tripping over mid scene
- Practise any **quick changes** that you have as soon as possible in rehearsal once the costume is available. The more times you do it the safer it will be.

Making costumes:

Remember that you don't have to personally make the costumes you design. But, if you do:

- Make sure that you are aware of how the sewing machine works – get someone to show you if you're not sure. You don't want to end up stitching yourself to the costume.
- Make sure you remove all pins from a costume before letting an actor try it on.

During performance:

You may not need to be involved with the costume at all during performance but if you do need to help backstage with quick changes or assisting the actor with accessories before the performance starts:

- Make sure that the backstage area is clear so that no-one trips over things in the dark
- Keep working areas tidy and if possible use a dim light so that you can check costumes before the actors go on stage.

Working as a lighting designer

Over the next few pages we will look at the role of a lighting designer, and the specific requirements for the different parts of your GCSE course should you wish to be assessed in this role.

What does a lighting designer do?

A lighting designer's job is one of the most important of all theatre jobs. After all, what's the point in the actors giving wonderful performances if they cannot be seen by the audience?

A lighting designer creates a world for the play by considering colour, brightness and direction of light; all of which help to create a sense of location and mood.

Like all of the technical roles, that of the lighting designer requires great skill in collaboration as it is their job to help to translate the ideas of the director into something realistic on stage.

So, for your GCSE what do **you** need to do as a lighting designer? Let's look at the specifics of what you need to do before exploring how to go about it:

Component 1: Devising

In this unit you would need to produce:

- A lighting design shown on a **grid plan** which uses at least four different types of **lantern**. This would show which lanterns you intend to use, where, and in what direction they would be focussed. You would also add information about choices of colours and accessories.
- A **lighting plot** or **cue sheet** which shows at least four different **lighting states** being used. This is the document that either you (if you're operating the lighting yourself) or your operator would use during the performance.
- You must supervise the **rigging** and **focussing** of your lights. Remember that it's your design you're being assessed on; not your ability to climb a ladder or to operate the lighting desk.
- You must be able to realise your design in performance which means that you must use your time effectively to create a lighting plan, rig it and run through the lighting with the actors all in time for the day.

Portfolio

Along with your practical work you need to keep a portfolio which is worth 45 marks. Your portfolio can be made up of notes, research, sketches, photographs and so on, just like a designer's notebook. You must also answer the following questions:

- What was your initial response to the stimuli and what were the intentions of the piece?
- What work did your group do in order to explore the stimuli and start to create ideas for performance?
- What were some of the significant moments during the development process and when rehearsing and refining your work?
- How did you consider **genre**, structure, character, form, style, and language throughout the process?
- How effective was your contribution to the final performance?
- Were you successful in what you set out to achieve?

THINKING ABOUT WORKING AS A DESIGNER?

Component 2: Performance from Text

To work as a lighting designer for this unit you need to do the following:

- If working as lighting designer on both extracts you must have produced a lighting plan using at least four different types of **lantern**
- Produce a **lighting plot** or **cue sheet** showing at least four changes in **lighting state** during the performance
- Supervise the **rigging** and **focussing** of your lighting design
- Realise your design in performance.

If you decide to work as a lighting designer for one extract and a performer for the second extract you only need to present a lighting design showing the use of **two** different types of lantern and **two** different lighting states must be seen in performance. Your lighting plot or cue sheet will still show the complete set of lighting changes for both extracts but the examiner will only expect to see two in action.

Where to start

If you are designing the lighting for a devised piece (component 1) then you need to spend some time in rehearsals as the play develops. This is to make sure that you are able to work collaboratively with the rest of your group, and that you know what kind of lighting is required. If designing for component 2 then you need to have read and studied the play which your extracts have come from.

Initial thoughts – ask the following questions:

- Where is the play set?
- What is the overall mood of the play or scenes – do they change? (Lighting is a great way of creating mood through colour and intensity.)
- Do the scenes need to be warm (oranges and reds) or cold (greens and blues)?
- What other colours might we want to use and why? (Consider themes in the play – can you show these through colour such as red for danger or passion?)

Developing your design – think about these questions:

- What types of lantern do I want to use and why?
- Where do I want to put them?
- What colours do I need to use?
- Do I need any accessories to make my plan work?
- When should the lighting change, and in what way? (Think about slow and quick fades.)
- Do I want to use **black outs** between scenes? You might find that it's more effective to dim the lights rather than go to black – this is often only used for a very large scene change.

WORKING AS A LIGHTING DESIGNER

Types of lantern

The largest number of lantern types that you need to be aware of is four, so here's a look at the most common ones:

Fresnel Spot

A really handy lantern which gives a nice soft edge to the light. It's good for using in a general wash across the acting space.

- A **barn door** can be fitted to a Fresnel to stop the main beam scattering onto bits of scenery
- The size of the beam can be adjusted with a screw mechanism.

Profile Spot

This lantern can produce a beam of light that has a hard or a soft edge. It has shutters which let you control the edge of the beam meaning that you can focus it down onto a smaller area. This lantern is good for spotlighting.

- A **gobo** can be fitted to this lantern to shape the beam of light.

Pebble Convex (PC)

This lantern is similar to the Fresnel, the main difference being that the lens has a pebble effect. This gives the beam of light a softer edge, but not as soft as a Fresnel.

- It also has an adjustable beam like the Fresnel.

PARcan

These lanterns are very good for using strong colours but not very good at general wash lighting because they are too powerful. PARcans would be good for special effects or for a very stylised moment within a play.

- These are also available as LED PARcans, which do not require gels and can be programmed for almost any colour.

PAR-16 (Birdie)

Your school might be lucky enough to have some of these tiny lights – or you could investigate how much it would cost to hire some. These little lights are great for hiding in bits of your set where no other light will fit. They produce bright, sharp edged pools of light.

THINKING ABOUT WORKING AS A DESIGNER?

Lighting Plan

Once you've decided which lights to use, you need to start to draw up a lighting plan like this one:

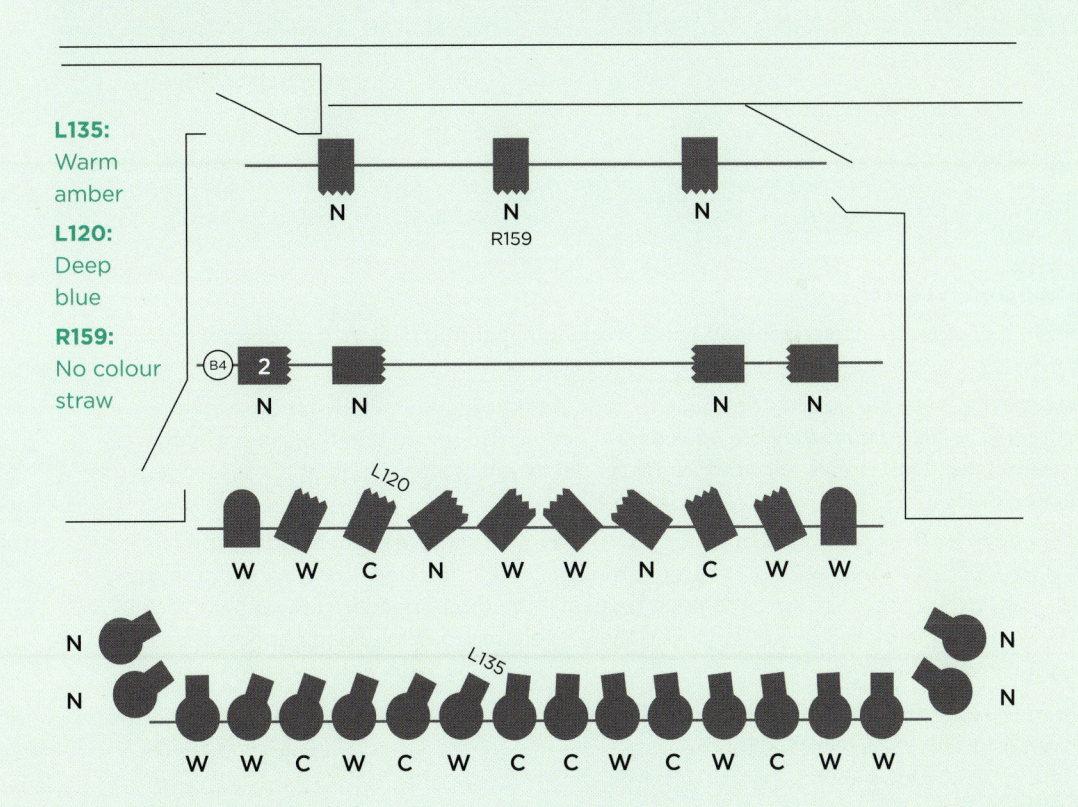

L135: Warm amber

L120: Deep blue

R159: No colour straw

Use the recognised symbols for each type of light:

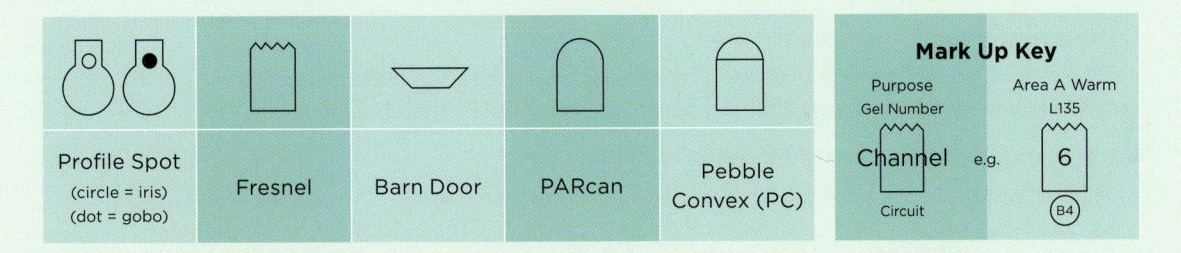

Profile Spot (circle = iris) (dot = gobo)	Fresnel	Barn Door	PARcan	Pebble Convex (PC)

Mark Up Key

Purpose / Gel Number — Channel — Circuit

Area A Warm — L135 — 6 — B4 — e.g.

Then write whether the beam of light will be warm, W, cool, C, or neutral, N. If you have a specific gel number in mind (Lee and Rosco make excellent gel filters and will often send samples) then you can write the number of the gel instead of W or C. Put L in front of the gel number for Lee, and R for Rosco. If you're using LED lights, there are no gel numbers to write down.

MAKING IT EASIER

It is possible to buy stencils of the symbols for the different lanterns, which makes drawing your plan much easier. Or, it is possible to find programmes on the internet that will help you to produce your plan electronically.

WORKING AS A LIGHTING DESIGNER

Lighting cue sheet

Your cue sheet should look like this:

Cue Number	Description	Cue point
Preset	General warm wash over whole of acting space.	On director's clearance before audience come in.
LXQ1	**Stage Left** door area brightens (over three seconds)	On Lydia's entrance – line 'I wasn't sure whether you'd be here or not.'

Inspiration and research

There are lots of ways to inspire yourself when working in lighting design. Try some of the following:

- A great starting point for lighting design is to look at photography. When a professional photographer takes a photo they are considering how to use the light in the same way that a lighting designer does. Books of photographs are an excellent starting point for learning about how light works.
- A good way to learn about angles in lighting is to play with some large heavy duty torches in a dark room. Look at what happens when the torch is held to the side, front, behind or even above a person. Try this with more than one torch at once (you'll need friends to help you), then try with a chair instead of a person. Use these exercises to help you to choose where you want your lanterns to hang.
- Go to the theatre and to concerts as much as possible to see lighting in action. Look at colours and think about moods that are created.

Health and safety

In all of your written work you will be required to show that you have taken notice of health and safety concerns. These might include:

During rigging and focussing:

It's likely that you won't be up a ladder yourself but you do need to show awareness of health and safety throughout your role as a lighting designer. You should write about this in your portfolio.

So, when rigging make sure the following has been done:

- Check that the ladder is extended properly if it's an **A Frame ladder**. Always 'foot' the ladder for the person who is rigging and check that all four feet of the ladder are on the floor.
- Don't overstretch when up a ladder – move the ladder instead.
- Use gloves if lanterns are being focussed – they will get hot.
- Make sure that all cables are neatly taped down and tidied away.
- Make sure each lantern that is rigged has a safety cable to stop anything falling down from the ceiling.

During the performance:

When operating the lighting board make sure that you or your operator takes note of these precautions:

- Don't have drinks or liquids near the lighting desk, because of the risk of electrocution
- Use a dim table lamp by the desk so that you (or your operator) can safely see what they are doing.

THINKING ABOUT WORKING AS A DESIGNER?

Working as a set designer

Over the next few pages we will look at the role of a set designer, and the specific requirements for the different parts of your GCSE course should you wish to be assessed in this role.

What does a set designer do?

A set designer's job is to create a physical world for the play which helps the audience to understand where the play is set. All of the scenery, **properties (props)** and furniture that an audience sees when they watch a play have been designed or chosen by the set designer.

So, for your GCSE what do **you** need to do as a set designer? Let's look at the specifics of what you need to do and then we can explore how to go about it:

Component 1: Devising

- You must make drawings of your final design including those of any important or relevant **props**.
- You need to create a **ground plan** of your set which shows where the entrances and exits are, where the furniture is located and where the audience will be seated.

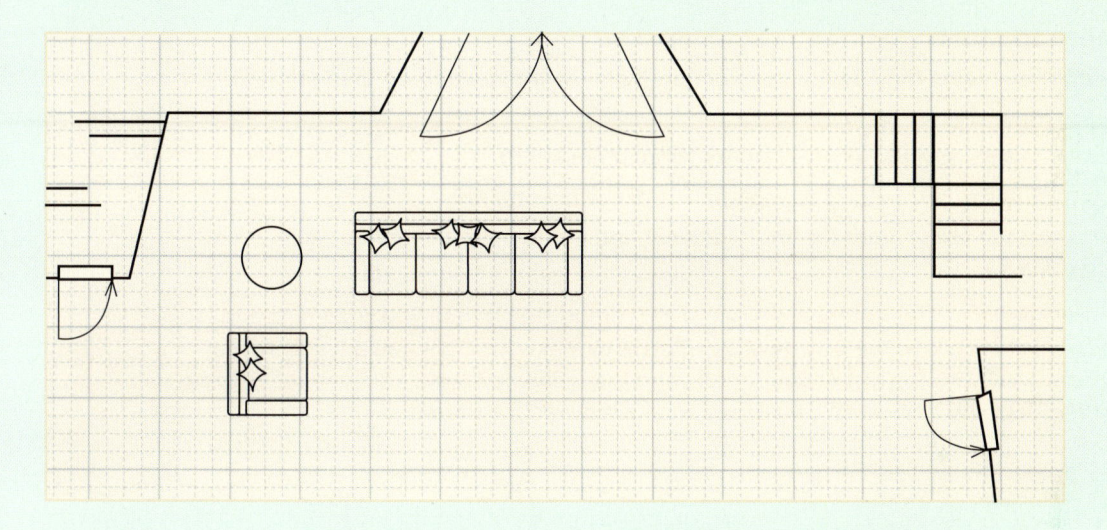

You need to supervise the making, hiring or borrowing of the materials for your set. Remember that it is your **design** that is being assessed, not your ability to hammer nails or paint a **backdrop**.

- There must be a realisation of your design in performance. In other words, you must have created something that the actors can act on or in.

Portfolio

Along with your practical work you need to keep a portfolio which is worth 45 marks. Your portfolio can be made up of notes, research, sketches, photographs and so on, just like a designer's notebook. You must also answer the following questions:

- What was your initial response to the stimuli and what were the intentions of the piece?
- What work did your group do in order to explore the stimuli and start to create ideas for performance?
- What were some of the significant moments during the development process and when rehearsing and refining your work?

- How did you consider **genre**, structure, character, form, style, and language throughout the process?
- How effective was your contribution to the final performance?
- Were you successful in what you set out to achieve?

Component 2: Performance from Text

To work as a set designer for this unit you need to do the following:

- Produce drawings of your final set design including any important props or furniture.
- Produce a ground plan showing the location of the audience, entrances and exits, and the location of furniture.
- Supervise the construction of your set by hiring, making or borrowing suitable materials. You do not have to make the set yourself.
- There must be a realisation of your design in performance.

If you decide to work as a set designer for one extract and a performer for the second extract you still need to present all of the above for both performances. In many circumstances the set may be the same for the two extracts.

For both components you need to show an awareness of health and safety.

Where to start

Whether your set is for a devised or a scripted play, it will need to do the following:

- suggest the style of the play
- create mood and atmosphere (just like lighting or sound)
- give clues as to the specific time and place of the action
- offer creative possibilities for the movement and grouping of the actors (think about using levels).

If you are designing the set for a devised play (component 1) then you need to spend lots of time in rehearsals as the play develops. This is to make sure that you are able to work collaboratively with the rest of your group, and that you know what your set needs to be used for, including how much back stage area is required for the actors.

Ask the following questions:

- Where is the play set?
- What does the set need to do? (Think about entrances and exits.)
- What colours do I want to use and why? (Consider themes and moods.)
- How much space do the actors need for certain scenes or moments? (Watch what they're doing and keep this in mind as you design.)

If you are designing for component 2 then you need to read and study the play from which your extracts come. Again, ask the questions above. You will need to note down the following:

1. Time of day, location, season, historical period.
2. Any changes to set required?
3. Any specific props, scenery or furnishings required?

These headings are also helpful for component 1.

THINKING ABOUT WORKING AS A DESIGNER?

What can a set be made from?

There are many answers to this question in the modern theatre. Here are some popular choices:

Wooden **flats** which can be stood up and weighted down by **stage weights**. These can be painted and texture added to them to create a **backdrop** or to suggest elements of buildings or other locations. Often these can be recycled from previous productions and have new canvas added or repainted. It's worth asking at your school or local theatre.

Use of **rostra** and significant props. In modern theatre we have moved away from the traditional scene change where the lights go down and the scene physically changes. Many locations can be suggested by simple sets such as raised rostra and well chosen furniture.

There is a trend for theatres and dance companies to use projected backdrops onto a wall or **cyclorama** in place of painted ones. The good thing about this is that you can change the scene with a touch of a mouse rather than having to have a physical scene change.

Some plays work well with a **scaffolding shell** – especially those which are stylised (see the image of *Jane Eyre* at the National Theatre on page 35). Actors can move around the space and find their own levels – do be aware however of health and safety issues. Perhaps beg a scaffolding company to lend you some materials and get them to construct it for you.

Projected backdrop used in *City of Angels* at the Donmar Warehouse, 2014

Inspiration and research

There are lots of ways to inspire yourself when designing set. Try some of the following:

- Go to the theatre as much as you can and see lots of different plays. Look closely at how sets are being used.
- Photographs of stage productions can be helpful because you can see the actors within the acting space, and the details on the set and furniture. Use photos in books or online, never take any in the theatre – this is a copyright issue.
- Ask your local theatre if you can look at the set for their current production – ask lots of questions.
- Keep a notebook of ideas including drawings of patterns, shapes and furniture that you see from day to day. Or alternatively use Pinterest to draw up a **mood board**.
- Look through furniture catalogues for ideas.

Health and safety

In all of your written work you will be required to show that you have taken notice of health and safety concerns. These might include:

- Making sure that actors get used to the set before performance. Allow them to explore in full light first – that way they are less likely to trip or fall.
- Mark any sharp edges or steps with white tape that can be seen in the dark.
- Don't lift heavy objects on your own – always ask for help.
- Make sure all flats are correctly weighted with stage weights.

If using fabrics such as curtains you need to think about **fireproofing**. Draw your teacher's attention to this in advance so that they can get the material treated.

Working as a sound designer

Over the next few pages we will look at the role of a sound designer, and the specific requirements for the different parts of your GCSE course should you wish to be assessed in this role.

What does a sound designer do?

A sound designer is responsible for everything that an audience hears during a performance, whether that is music or sound effects. A sound designer works in a similar way to a set and lighting designer in that they must create the world of the play so that the audience understands where scenes are set, and what atmosphere is being created. These sounds may come from recorded or live sound, and we'll look at both later.

So, for your GCSE what do **you** need to do as a sound designer? Let's look at the specifics of what you need to do before exploring how to go about it:

Component 1: Devising

- Make a **source sheet** showing at least four different sound effects which can be a mixture of original, live or **found effects**.

- Make a **cue sheet** which shows where your sound effects will happen during the play, how long they run for, how loud they will be and what equipment they will be played on.

- Supervise the creation of your sound design. This means that you must decide what sound effects you want to use, but you can have help to record them to get just the effect you want.

- There must be a realisation of your design in performance. You do not necessarily need to operate the sound yourself. As long as the design is yours, you can ask someone else to operate it for you.

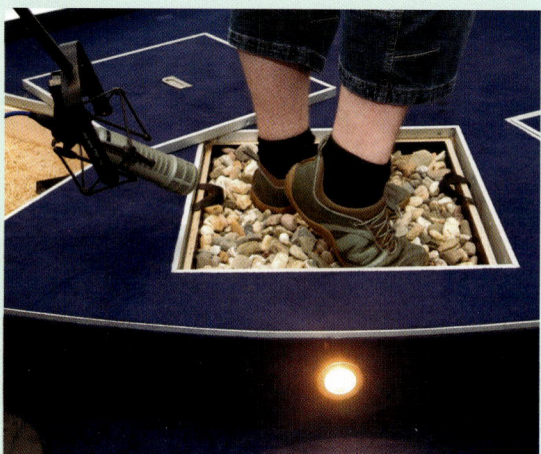

Portfolio

Along with your practical work you need to keep a portfolio which is worth 45 marks. Your portfolio can be made up of notes, research, sketches, photographs and so on, just like a designer's notebook.

You must also answer the following questions:

- What was your initial response to the stimuli and what were the intentions of the piece?
- What work did your group do in order to explore the stimuli and start to create ideas for performance?
- What were some of the significant moments during the development process and when rehearsing and refining your work?
- How did you consider **genre**, structure, character, form, style, and language throughout the process?
- How effective was your contribution to the final performance?
- Were you successful in what you set out to achieve?

THINKING ABOUT WORKING AS A DESIGNER?

Component 2: Performance from Text

To work as a sound designer for this unit you need to do the following:

- If working as sound designer on both extracts you must have a **source sheet** showing 4 different sound cues
- Produce a **cue sheet** for both performances
- Supervise the creation of your final sound design
- Your sound must be realised in performance.

If you decide to work as a sound designer for one extract and a performer for the second extract you only need to present a source sheet showing 2 sound cues for assessment rather than two. Your cue sheet will still cover all the other sounds required for the extracts.

For both components you need to show an awareness of health and safety factors.

Where to start

Whether your sound is for a devised piece or a scripted play, it will need to do the following:

- Suggest the location of the play (for example use of birdsong or waves to show an outdoor location)
- Create mood and atmosphere (think about how music is used in TV drama and films)
- Create specific sound effects such as gun shots or doorbells.

If you are designing the sound for a devised piece (component 1) then you need to spend lots of time in rehearsals as the play develops. This is to make sure that you are able to work collaboratively with the rest of your group by discussing what sounds are required, and what else is happening in those scenes. It also gives you the chance to try out some sounds and see if they work.

If you are designing for component 2 then you need to read and study the play that your extracts come from. Make a list of all the sounds that are definitely needed in the extracts. These will usually be given in the stage directions, but also sometimes in the dialogue, for example:

```
JOHN: Did you hear a bird just then?
MARY: No, I wasn't listening.
JOHN: Listen, there it is again.
MARY: That's not a bird.
```

In this extract there are no stage directions to tell us that we need the sound of a bird. However, what the characters say gives us the information. Sometimes you need to be a detective – is John actually hearing a bird or is Mary right? Is it something else? In these situations, talk to your director, or the group if you are devising, about what kind of sound they have in mind.

Where can I find sound effects?

- There are plenty of CDs available which have compilations of commonly used sound effects. Often they are grouped into categories such as traffic (cars, buses, planes and so on), entertainment (crowd noises, clinking glasses) or military (gunshots, tanks). These CDs are a good starting point.
- There are lots of websites where you can download free sound effects as MP3 or WAV files. Using a search engine for these will give you plenty of choice.

What if I can't find what I want?

There is always the fun option of recording your own sound effects. All you need is a good hand-held recording device that will produce MP3s, a couple of different microphones and lots of random objects that you can use to make noise. You could decide to perform some of these sounds live during the performance. This is known as **foley**.

Here are some examples of how you can create your own sound effects:

- A tray of gravel or cat litter can produce excellent footstep noises
- Beanbags can be used to create all sorts of different sounds, particularly waves
- Ripping and rustling a crisp packet can sound like lighting a match or starting a fire
- Dried peas in a box can sound like rain.

The trick with this is to experiment and to really start to listen to the sounds around you. Often the most effective sound effects are not made by the actual object!

What other equipment will be used?

The specification from the exam board states that you should have access to the following:

- A sound reproduction system – for example speakers, a CD player or laptop.
- A mixing desk – to allow you to use more than one channel and to fade in and out.
- Two types of microphone – sound effects and speech require different types. Try a dynamic moving coil, a **cardioid**, or a condenser microphone and a shield to stop unwanted sounds like wind when recording outside or 'popping' on vocal consonants such as the letter 'p'.
- Access to sound sources (pre-recorded sound effects).

It's also helpful to have access to Audacity (a free software programme where you can record and edit) and Q-Lab (another free programme) which allows you to load in your cues in order, ready for performance.

Paperwork

Sound source sheet

This just shows what cues you are using, and where the sound is coming from. For example:

Cue number and description	Source
Q1 Telephone ringing	Pre-recorded – CD BBC Sound Effects
Q2 Rain outside	Peas in box (foley)
Q3 Music for scene change	Own composition – recorded on Audacity

THINKING ABOUT WORKING AS A DESIGNER?

Sound Cue Sheet

No. of cue	Page in script	Type of cue	Level	Length	Distribution
Q1	3	**Spot cue**	10	5 secs, then stops when answered **visual cue**	Laptop through Q Lab
Q2	10	Spot cue	20	6 secs	Live (foley)
Q3	15	Fade in	Up to 25	Fade out once scene change is complete	Laptop through Q Lab

DO YOU KNOW YOUR CUES?

Some useful theatre terminology to help you decide how your sound should be used:

Spot cue: These are cues that happen at specific moments in a play like a telephone ringing, or a doorbell.

Visual cue: This is when the operator needs to watch the stage to either start or stop a cue. For example, needing to stop the telephone ringing as soon as it is picked up.

Fade in: When a sound cue starts at a low volume which increases slowly. Fades can go up or down.

Inspiration and research

- Lots of inspiration will come from actually listening to the world around you – really take note of what things sound like
- When you're watching the TV or a film, tune into the kind of music that has been used and think about why it's been chosen
- Listen to radio plays to see how sound effects have been used.

Health and safety

As much of what you will do as a sound designer relies on electricity, be careful when working with equipment:

- Always tape down lose cables so that people don't trip over them
- Never have drinks near the sound equipment
- Don't play sounds at unnaturally high volumes – you could damage your own or other people's hearing
- Don't lift or carry anything too heavy – ask for help.

Glossary

Apron stage. If part of the stage extends beyond the proscenium arch and in front of the curtain towards the audience, it is called an apron stage.

Aristotle's *Poetics*. Written by the ancient Greek philosopher Aristotle in about 335BC, *Poetics* is the earliest surviving book on dramatic theory, and includes the philosopher's definition of a tragedy and his description of 'tragic pleasure' or catharsis.

Aside. When an actor breaks the 'fourth wall' to speak briefly to the audience directly – usually with the theatrical convention that other characters on stage with them do not notice them doing so.

Backdrop. The wall or screen, painted as set or not, which stands at the back of a performance space.

Barn door. In lighting, an attachment fitted to the front of a Fresnel lantern, with four rigid adjustable flaps which can be positioned to shape the beam of light and shade it, for example, to prevent it scattering or shining in the eyes of the audience.

Beat. A short pause in dialogue, often marked as a stage direction in the text. Shorter than the direction 'pause'.

Birdie. In lighting, the common nickname for a PAR-16: a very small variety of PARcan, run from a transformer rather than through the lighting rig.

Black out. Technical term, often written in scripts at ends of scenes or whole plays, to indicate that all stage lights should be turned off: usually immediately, and distinguishable from 'fade to black' which is more gradual.

Blank verse. The poetic form in which much of Shakespeare is written, and many other dramatic texts. Blank verse refers to unrhymed lines of iambic pentameter. 10 syllables in a line, divided into patterns of 5 paired unstressed and stressed syllables: 'de-DUM', for example Orsino's opening line in *Twelfth Night*: 'If MUsic BE the FOOD of LOVE, play ON'

Cardioid microphone. The most common form of unidirectional microphone: often used for vocal recording as it is good at filtering out external sounds from directions other than the voice speaking or singing into it.

Catharsis. Aristotle's concept of 'tragic pleasure': a form of purification which comes of the purging of emotion through art. We experience catharsis when watching characters suffer in dramatic tragedies.

Centre stage. In the middle of the stage.

Commedia dell'Arte. An Italian form of theatre which began in the 16th century and featured a number of stock character types. See page 49 for further information.

Context. Very important when studying and rehearsing drama, context to be gathered can include information on the historical period in which a play was *written*, is *set*, and the context of the time in which it will be *received* by audiences today. Contextual information is important to the characters actors play – in terms of who they are, their background and life stories, and important for the director and designers to consider in their production decisions.

Costume plot. A complete list of all the characters in a play and the details of their costumes, including any necessary costume changes.

Cross-cutting. Incorporating flashbacks or flash-forwards at intervals in a plot, so that the story is not told in a linear way.

Cross-garters. A fashion for wrapping pairs of ribbons around the legs, crossed over at intervals, briefly popular during the Elizabethan period and ridiculed in Shakespeare's *Twelfth Night*.

Cue sheet. A document which lays out all the 'cues' in a play: this applies to lighting and to sound cues and notes at what moment each sound or lighting change happens, how long it goes on for, how loud (in the case of sound) and what equipment is used to create it.

Cyclorama (cyc). A large curtain, sheet or screen on which lighting or images can be projected, often used as a backdrop, and sometimes concave in shape.

Diaphragm. One of the actor's most important muscles. Umbrella-shaped and located beneath the lungs.

Direct address. The term used when an actor speaks directly to the audience, breaking the 'fourth wall'.

Downstage. Near the front of the stage: towards the audience.

Emotional memory. A technique which forms part of Stanislavski's 'system' and requires an actor to recall moments of their own emotional past in order to find emotion in a character.

Farce. Highly exaggerated and improbable comedy, usually very fast-paced and incorporating visual humour, and often slapstick, mistaken identity, and a degree of licentiousness.

Fireproofing. An essential part of stage health and safety: most things can be fireproofed with a special spray.

Flash-back/flash-forward. When the usual linear progression of time in a plot is broken to show a scene or a moment from the past or future of the characters involved.

Flats. Flat, upright pieces of stage scenery, usually made of wood, which either self-support or are secured with stage-weights, and can be painted to look like walls or whole buildings.

Focussing. The act of choosing the length and position of beams of light.

Foley. Sound effects, produced live or pre-recorded, but created by the sound designer, such as shaking a large metal sheet to produce the sound of thunder and lightning, or walking in a tray of gravel.

Forum theatre. A form of politically motivated theatre developed by Augusto Boal in which the audience were 'spect-actors' expected to interrupt and contribute to the action by making suggestions about which direction it should go in.

Found effects. Sound effects which are found rather than created through foley.

Fourth wall. The imaginary wall which has been 'removed' so that the audience can see the action of the play.

Fresnel spot. Form of lantern often used to give a general wash of light across a space.

Genre. A type of theatre, for example 'comedy', 'tragedy', 'farce', 'political drama'.

Grid plan. A lighting design plan showing what types of lights are to be used in a production, where they'll be placed, focussed in what direction, and also noting any accessories to be used with them.

Ground plan. A bird's-eye plan of the set, showing the position of entrances, furniture and so on.

Hot seating. A form of improvisation used to develop character: the actor, in role, is asked questions by other members of the cast or director.

Improvisation. Non-scripted performance.

Inflection. Alteration in pitch, volume or tone of voice.

Jacobean. Of the time of King James I: immediately after the Elizabethan period, and in the later part of Shakespeare's career.

Lantern. A stage light, usually suspended above or affixed at the sides of the stage and auditorium to shine on the action.

Lighting plot. See 'cue sheet'.

Lighting state. The combination of lights being used at any one time.

LXQ1, 2, 3…etc. The shorthand used on a cue sheet for lighting cues, numbered in order of appearance.

Mixing desk. An electronic board of switches and sliders for combining and altering the levels or tone of sounds: music or sound effects.

Monologue. A speech of some length (more than a few sentences) spoken by a single actor.

Mood board. A design stimulus: physical or digital, a collection of images, scraps of colour, perhaps fabrics, placed together on a pinboard as an underlying thematic plan for a design.

Movement sequence. Usually silent, accompanied by movement or narration, the telling of a story through movement (not necessarily dance) alone.

Naturalism. Late 19th century movement in theatre to create drama which is as close as possible to reality.

Objective. A character's overarching aim within a section or unit of a scene: what they want to happen.

PARcan. Powerful lantern, good for strong colours.

Pebble Convex (PC). Lantern similar to a Fresnel but with a 'pebbled' lens.

Personification. Giving human characteristics to a non-human object or abstract idea.

Physical theatre. A form of theatre in which movement or physicality plays a strong part in the telling of the story.

Plant. In theatre, a member of the cast who is placed within the audience without the audience knowing that they are actually part of the acting company.

Preset. A lighting state, prop, item of furniture or actor who is in position on stage before the performance begins.

Profile spot. A type of lantern often used for spotlighting.

Projection. In acting, speaking in a voice which is well supported by the diaphragm and therefore carries well to the audience with volume.

Proscenium arch. Literally 'in front of the scenery', the name given to the arch which separates the stage from the audience, and the most common form of West-End theatre layout.

Properties (props). Objects such as books, cups, bottles, skateboards, walking sticks, when used on stage: referred to as 'personal props' if they are only used by one particular actor/character.

Proxemics. The study of spatial distances between human beings: in theatre between the characters on stage and also between performers and audience, and how that affects the way in which each feel during a performance.

Quick change. A costume change which must be performed quickly – often in a designated 'quick change' area backstage if there isn't time for the performer to return to their dressing room.

Rigging. The process of securing lights and also the name for the structure to which the lanterns are secured, often suspended above the stage and/or auditorium: a 'lighting rig'.

Role on the wall. A character development technique in which words or phrases which describe the character are written into the outline of a body and hung on the wall of the rehearsal space: often a collaborative process.

Rostra (rostrum). Raised platforms on which performers can stand, often placed on stage and connected together in groups to create levels.

Satire. A genre in which vices or follies prevalent in real life are ridiculed: sub-genres include social satire and political satire.

Scaffolding shell. A non-naturalistic approach to set design in which levels and interest are created for performers to move over, without painted scenery or flats.

Site-specific theatre. Drama performed somewhere other than a standard theatre, such as in a park or an abandoned warehouse: particularly when the site is connected directly to the setting of the narrative, such as a pirate story being performed on a ship.

Slapstick. Named after a prop which used to be used in farces: a paddle which makes a loud whacking sound, slapstick now refers to a genre of exaggerated physical comedy in which characters often fall over or otherwise appear to hurt themselves.

Soliloquy. The word often used for a Shakespearean monologue where a character is speaking to the audience or to themselves, rather than to another character on stage. 'To be or not to be...' is perhaps the world's most famous soliloquy.

Soundscape. A combination of sounds which creates the sense of an environment.

Source sheet. A table prepared by a sound designer to show what sounds are being used in a production, organised by cue number, and where they are to come from (their 'source').

Split focus. When two different scenes or dialogues are occurring simultaneously on stage.

Spot cue. Cues which happen at specific moments in a play, such as a doorbell.

Stage left. Best thought of as 'actor's left' – this is actually the right hand side of the stage as the audience looks at it.

Stage right. As above, 'actor's right', or the left hand side of the stage from the audience perspective.

Stage weights. Used to secure flats or other parts of set and scenery, these are extremely heavy and should be lifted with care.

Stance. The way in which an actor stands in role, affected by things such as the age and personality of their character.

Still image. When actors create a photograph-like still image, rather than moving about the stage.

Stimulus. Anything which helps to stimulate creative ideas: a stimulus can be, for example, a sound, word, or a colour.

Stock characters. Used in genres of theatre such as Commedia del'Arte or Melodrama, standard repeated characters who can be found in various forms across a number of different works, such as the wily servant, the deaf old man, the villainous master, and so on.

Tableau. A technique in creative drama in which performers create a frozen picture, as if the action were paused; plural is tableaux. See and 'still image'.

Tallescope. A telescopic aluminium platform used for working at height, fixing lights, for example.

Tension. The key to almost any good drama. That which stands between characters and each other or that which arises from their struggle to achieve their objectives.

Theatre in the round. When the performance space is surrounded by audience on all sides.

Thrust stage. Where the stage space extends into the audience so that they are placed on three sides of it.

Tragedy. As defined by Aristotle in his *Poetics*, a story of human suffering with a tragic hero (or heroine) which evokes 'catharsis'.

Traverse. A stage layout where the audience sits on two sides of the stage, facing each other: like a fashion catwalk.

Unit. A small subsection of a scene which holds together as representing a distinct moment of action, where perhaps a character is pursuing a particular objective, or a particular topic is being discussed.

Upstage. Towards the back of the stage, away from the audience.

Verbatim theatre. A play written using the actual words of people interviewed, or built from correspondence, to tell a true story using real-life accounts of its events.

Visual cue. A cue for a lighting or sound effect which comes not from the dialogue but from an action performed by a character on stage: for example, a sound operator must watch for an actor to pick up a telephone as the cue to stop the sound effect of it ringing.

Wings. The areas to each side of the stage, obscured from the audience's view by the proscenium arch.

Index

1984 . . . . 67, 117-126

Alexander technique 24

An Inspector Calls 67, 68-76

Blue Stockings 67, 127-136

Boal, Augusto 29, 173

Brecht, Bertolt 46

Cardboard Citizens 29

Commedia del'Arte . . . .
49, 53, 172, 175

Costume . . . .
13, 35, 38-39, 47, 50, 59, 65,
74-75, 84-85, 94-95, 103-104,
114-115, 123, 129, 133, 143, 147,
149, 151, 154-159, 172, 174

Cross-cutting 26, 172

The Crucible 67, 77-87

Design . . . .
6-7, 39, 65, 76, 85, 87, 95, 97,
103-104, 106-107, 115-116, 123-124,
126, 133-134, 136, 144, 146,
149-150, 154-171

Devised theatre . . . .
12-45, 156-157, 161, 166, 169

DNA 67, 108-116

Dr Korczak's Example . 67, 137-146

Forum theatre 29, 173

Frantic Assembly 15, 20, 22

Government Inspector . . . 67, 88-97

Health and Safety . . . .
34-35, 38-39, 44, 159, 164,
166-167, 169, 171, 173

Historical theatre styles . . . .
8-10, 20, 46, 62, 103-104,
172-173, 175

Hot seating 18, 26, 173

Improvisation . . . .
19, 22, 26, 49, 173

Kneehigh 12, 15

Lighting . . . .
11, 13, 34, 39, 47, 65, 76, 87, 97,
107, 116, 126, 136, 146, 150-152,
154-156, 160-164, 172-175

Live theatre evaluation . . . .
66-67, 147-153

Macbeth 48, 58-64

Monologue 48, 58-64, 174

Movement and physical theatre . .
17-19, 51, 174

Naturalism . . . .
9, 20, 115-116, 150, 174

One Man, Two Guvnors 49-57

Performance (assessed) 36-38

Portfolio (component 1) . . . .
13-15, 17, 27, 34-36, 39, 40-45,
154, 156, 160, 164-165, 168

Promenade theatre 11, 28

Proxemics . . . .
18, 41, 50-51, 59-60, 125,
133-134, 143-144, 148, 174

Punchdrunk 15, 28

Rehearsal . . . .
5-7, 12-35, 32-33, 37-38, 40-41,
45-46, 48, 50, 56, 59, 65, 155-157,
159-160, 166, 168-169, 172

Research . . . .
7, 12, 15, 17, 19, 22, 26-29, 34,
40-42, 45, 74-6, 84, 87, 94, 97,
103, 107, 114, 116, 123, 126, 133,
136, 143, 146, 155-156, 158, 160,
164-165, 167-168, 171

Revision . . . .
7, 66, 70, 74, 79, 84, 90, 94,
100, 103, 110, 114, 119, 123, 129,
133, 139, 143, 151

Role on the wall 30, 174

Set . . . .
3, 6, 32, 39, 47, 65-66, 74,
76, 84, 87, 94-95, 97, 103-107,
114, 116, 123, 126-127, 129, 133,
135-137, 139, 143-144, 146-147,
150-151, 153-156, 165-167,
172-175

Site-specific theatre 11, 28, 174

Sound . . . .
6, 13, 14, 16, 22, 25, 35, 39, 47,
60, 65, 76, 87, 97, 107, 112, 116,
126, 147, 149, 151, 153, 154-155,
168-171, 172-175

Staging types . . . .
8-9, 10-11, 85, 95, 104, 134, 144,
150, 172, 174-175

Stanislavski, Konstantin . . . .
9, 20, 30-31, 54, 173

Tableau 17-18, 29, 173, 175

The Woman in Black . . . .
147, 149-150

Tragedy . . . .
8-9, 20, 59-60, 172-173, 175

Twelfth Night 67, 98-107

Verbatim theatre 26-27, 175

Voice . . . .
10, 20, 22-24, 38, 50-51, 57,
59-60, 73, 75-76, 83, 86-87,
95-97, 102-106, 112, 115, 118,
123, 125, 129, 132, 134-135, 143,
145, 148, 172-174